The Ever Changing Sky

The Ever Changing Sky

Meditations on the Psalms

Edward Francisco

RESOURCE *Publications* • Eugene, Oregon

THE EVER CHANGING SKY
Meditations on the Psalms

Copyright © 2021 Edward Francisco. All rights reserved. Except for brief quotations in critical publications or reviews, no part of this book may be reproduced in any manner without prior written permission from the publisher. Write: Permissions, Wipf and Stock Publishers, 199 W. 8th Ave., Suite 3, Eugene, OR 97401.

Resource Publications
An Imprint of Wipf and Stock Publishers
199 W. 8th Ave., Suite 3
Eugene, OR 97401

www.wipfandstock.com

PAPERBACK ISBN: 978-1-7252-7553-9
HARDCOVER ISBN: 978-1-7252-7554-6
EBOOK ISBN: 978-1-7252-7555-3

JUNE 17, 2021

For my wife

Linda

and my sons

Robert, Erik and Gabriel

With love

Contents

Preface | ix

Note on Translation | xi

MEDITATIONS ON THE PSALMS | 1

Postface | 263

Bibliography | 265

Preface

Thirteen years ago, in early middle age, I embarked upon a quest to read the Psalms and write a series of meditations on them. Little did I know what I was getting started. I'd read the Psalms, of course—numerous times, dating to my childhood. I was aware of other people's commentaries and meditations on them. I referred to selected Psalms often in the college course I taught called *Christology: Images of Jesus*. However, I had never taken the time to live with them or let them live in me. That was a much bigger undertaking.

Through the agency of the Psalms, I was forced to see ordinary events in my life—husbanding, parenting, teaching—through the lens of the extraordinary, magnified and in sharp relief. The middle years are a terrifying period for many people. The corridor of time narrows to a fixed point on the horizon. Choices shrink; regrets loom large. Lost possibilities are punctuated by the mocking laughter of the devil. The self that a person spends a lifetime becoming suddenly seems diaphanous and unreal.

The poet John Keats said that life is an arena of soul making. If so, then part of the soul's work is to acquire authenticity over time. In a similar vein, Trappist monk Thomas Merton once said that a saint is someone who is most him or herself—fully human. If I've learned one thing living with the Psalms during the period, it's that I'm no saint but am all too human. Doubtlessly my flaws are writ large in these meditations. Complexities, tensions, and contradictions inseparable from the human condition are here, too. If I've gleaned another thing from my *lectio divina*, or sacred reading of the Psalms, it is that the Psalmist, too, was aware of such things, experiencing the full range of human emotions. It is comforting to know that Jesus himself experienced this spectrum of feeling, living, as he did, in the fullness of humanity. The awful contradictions of the cross are those perplexities and paradoxes that each of us is called to recognize within ourselves and to forgive in others.

Under no circumstance did I want these meditations to be pious reflections. They are not a how-to work of devotion either. They reflect a journey of fits and starts and much hard work on the part of the Holy Spirit. I don't expect anyone to read them at one sitting. I certainly didn't write them that way. They can be read out of order because that's how they were written. I also tend to focus on one verse in each psalm that had special meaning for me at the time of my reading. Despite these qualifications, what I hope the reader finds in these meditations is an oratorio of pain, love, and possibility—requirements of a shared human journey.

I am now in late middle age. The children I wrote about are grown and gone. My vocation as a college teacher will soon end. Many of my friends have already retired. Some have died. Those of us living talk more about the past than about what is ahead of us. What lies before us, in the poet's words, are "vast deserts of eternity." That is the circumstance I encountered thirteen years ago. The only difference is a discovery I made along the way. It is in the desert where possibility blooms. My ultimate hope is that these meditations speak to what is authentic in all of us.

Note on Translation

As a literary historian and professor of Shakespeare, I have selected the King James translation of the psalms as inspiration for *The Ever Changing Sky*. My reasons are several. First, the King James Bible (KJV) is universally regarded as the most poetic of all the translations. Such books as Job, Psalms, Proverbs, and the Song of Songs are full of poetic features, including rich imagery, sonorous rhythms, and mesmeric repetitions. It stands to reason that the KJV, as the King James version is abbreviated, was the work of learned scholars at the pinnacle of the Jacobean poetic and dramatic traditions. In short, the forty-seven translators appointed by King James stood in the lineage of literary succession that included Francis Bacon, John Donne, Ben Jonson, and William Shakespeare, luminaries who bestowed on the English language unprecedented privilege.

The second reason for choosing the King James version is that it is essentially a literal translation. The translators did not act as interpreters, but rather as translators. They wished to produce an authentic text. To that purpose, translators chose the words they did because they believed the words they chose were the most accurate ones. Also, when we consider that for modern publishers of the Bible, a new translation must be considered significantly different from the original in order to receive a copyright, we can be certain that the KJV requires no copyright because it is the original text.

Finally, my choice of the KVJ derives, in part, from the knowledge that its translators were authorities on Hebrew, Greek, and Latin and such cognate languages as Aramaic, Syriac, and Arabic. In Elizabethan and Jacobean grammar schools, students were expected to show mastery of Latin, Greek, Hebrew, and English. Working from the Vulgate Bible, translators proved their proficiency in translating Latin into English.

Note on Translation

A final note: because of the time since its first printing, the KJV is in the public domain, and people using it do not have to seek permission to use it. Note, too, that each meditation for each psalm begins with a verse from that psalm. All other biblical quotations in the meditation will derive from the same psalm unless otherwise indicated.

Psalm 1

"Blessed is the man that walketh not in the counsel of the ungodly, nor standeth in the way of sinners, nor sitteth in the seat of the scornful. But his delight is in the law of the Lord . . ." (Ps 1:1–2a)

Catholic novelist Walker Percy expresses a feature of middle-aged despair when he talks about being caught between two types of people in his midst: believers who are intolerable and unbelievers who are insane.[1] I encountered the first variety today at Mass in the person of a young priest named Chris who longs for the good old days of the sixteenth century when religious wars separated the faithful from the infidels.

In his defense he's young, but I'm afraid he's going to do horrific damage before life's vicissitudes have an opportunity to impart to him a smattering of humility. Today's homily unfortunately took place on July 4, Independence Day in the United States, giving him an opportunity to combine religion and jingoism in equal measures of intolerance. Distorting history, making it conspire with his own distorted views, he even resurrected the specter of communism, the "Red Devil" as he termed it, stating that we had a duty to oppose such evil, godless systems, the way the Founding Fathers fought the British. Obviously the young man's confusions were legion.

To see the old patterns of hatred, rigidity, and intolerance repeated in a new generation of the young is, unfortunately, one of the sad by-products of living to middle-age and beyond. The hope exists that the young priest will live to such a time in his own life when his certainties are shattered, his words are seen as platitudes, and his cherished laws are felt as swords cleaving a wound of compassion for others. According to St. John of the Cross, confusion, suffering, and grief are secret ways God frees us from our

---

1. Percy, *Second Coming*, 90.

attachments and idolatries, bringing us to the realization of our true nature. Let that nature be manifest in all of us with each day's passing.[2]

---

2. Green and Stump, *Hidden Divinity*, 227–77.

Psalm 2

"Why do the heathen rage, and the people imagine a vain thing?"
(Ps 2:1)

I have a habit of attempting to discover what I term the hidden souls of words. This search involves finding cognates, or etymological and phonetic variations, revealing associations and hidden layers of meaning among words not immediately obvious. For example, the word *Mary* or the phrase *Age of Mary* might produce the following:

- mer
- mere
- meru
- mero
- mare
- merry + age
- marry + age
- marriage

The above list reveals only a few of the associations generated by the word *Mary*, which has its roots in the Latin *mare*, or sea. The Virgin Mary is sometimes referred to as Mary Star of the Sea because of her close connection with fishermen, the fishers of men described by St. Matthew. Jesus, too, was said to be born under the sign of Pisces, or the fish. Constellation of meanings pertinent to this psalm might derive from the word *vain*:

- vane
- vein

- venial
- veneer
- venture
- Venus
- Venous

Although the pattern here may be a bit more complex to decipher, the key, again, seems to reside in the Latin root of the word *vanus* meaning empty.

In his book *The Dark Night of the Soul*, Gerald G. May describes the point in our middle years when all our vain hopes, aspirations, and ambitions are revealed:

> Perhaps the career we worked so hard to achieve is not as rewarding as we'd expected. Maybe the love relationship we thought would make us complete has become timeworn and frayed. Things that gave us pleasure in the past may now seem empty. Such glimpses occur in unique ways for each person, but they always happen. They happen repeatedly. Each time, they represent a twilight of the dark night of the soul.[1]

May's allusion to St. John of the Cross's dark night of the soul alerts us to the certainty that we can only postpone the time of reckoning and realization facing us:

> Early in life it is often possible to shut out these momentary dissatisfactions as soon as they appear. We can blame them on a bad mood, tough circumstances, or a lousy day. We can assume things will be better tomorrow.[2]

However, as May notes,

> In the middle of life, we begin to sense our time is limited; changes need to be more radical if we're going to find what we want before we're too old to enjoy it. Still later in life we may finally be more open to acceptance. Perhaps what we've been after all along have been only appetizers, "messengers." Maybe we've been grasping for good things when what we've really desired is the Creator of all good things.[3]

---

1. May, *Dark Night*, 63.
2. May, *Dark Night*, 63.
3. May, *Dark Night*, 64.

Psalm 2

Speaking for myself, the sense of loss and attendant depression are agonizing at times, especially when I resist letting go of what no longer exists, the vain imaginings described by the Psalmist. In fact, I think I'd go insane, at times, were it not for St. John's assurance that, while I can't navigate the desert, God can.

Psalm 3

"I laid me down and slept; I awaked; for the Lord sustained me."
(Ps 3:5)

I told my wife that I dread sleeping. Lately my dreams have seemed less like dreams and more like a surreal quest into an actual landscape littered with all sorts of terrifying presences: "ten thousands of people that have set themselves against me round about." I'm not exaggerating when I say that the place to which I go each night is like an actual world, and I almost always find myself in the midst of a battle there against overwhelming forces.

    I am familiar with much of the psychoanalytic literature concerning dreams and how terrors by day can transform into arrows that fly by night. In other words, dreaming is sometimes a way of solving conscious problems unconsciously. Those worries that afflict us in our waking hours don't simply go away when we lay our heads to rest on the pillow.

    Nevertheless, there is something qualitatively different about the sorts of dream I'm having at this time in my life. For one thing, I am often visited in my dreams by two old friends, both dead at an early age. They are usually allies in the battles I'm supposed to fight. Oftentimes, however, I find myself ineffectual, the chaos overwhelming. Too, I experience the uneasy sensation that I'm not sure on which side I should be fighting. My moral compass no longer seems to work.

    A priest friend said to me a few weeks ago: "Getting old is not for sissies." He couldn't have spoken truer words. My mind immediately goes to Alfred, Lord Tennyson's poem "Ulysses," which finds the aging king recalling his former heroic exploits and the deeds of noble warriors long since laid in the dust. Though Ulysses acknowledges that "I am all that I have met," he intuits, too, what lies ahead: "Yet all experience is an arch wherethro' / Gleams that untravell'd world, whose margin fades / For ever and forever when I move." The sense of arriving at the end of things pervades every line of the poem but one. That line shows Ulysses longing for a "bringer of new things."[1] That is surely the wish of a man tired of seeing life piled on life and who is seeking what he mercifully knows can't be found within himself.

---

1. Tennyson, "Ulysses," 19–21.

Psalm 4

"Hear me when I call, O God of my righteousness: though hast enlarged me when I was in distress: have mercy upon me and hear my prayer." (Ps 4:1)

I'm offering a new course at my college entitled "Introduction to Shakespeare." I'm now asking myself in frustration: "What have you done to yourself?" Only a fool, or someone consumed with *hubris*, would take on such a task. A person could meditate on Shakespeare's works for eternity. They're like the Christian scriptures in that way. I'm beginning to think of Shakespeare not as a man, but as a supernatural or mythical being, like one of the Titans of old, one of the pillars of civilization. Yet, the bard is remarkably human in his ability to convey the full range of human passions, no better demonstrated than in his play *King Lear*, the story of an aging king who gives his kingdom to his daughters only to discover that two of his three offspring are willing to betray him. The play is a mirror of the human condition in almost every way imaginable. At the core of the drama is the question: How much control do we have over ourselves and others? How much choice do we have in determining the direction and outcome of our lives? I'm beginning to believe not much.

Finding parallels between Lear and the biblical Adam, the brilliant literary critic Northrop Frye states that "the tragedy of Adam, the archetypal human tragedy, resolves, like all other tragedies, in the manifestation of natural law. He enters a world in which existence is itself tragic, not existence modified by an act, deliberate or unconscious."[1] I take Frye's comment to mean that all choice takes place in a context of limitations experienced by everyone. There is no escaping this situation. Frye goes on to say that existence is tragic in *King Lear* because existence is inseparable

---

1. Frye, *King Lear*, 15.

from relation; we are born from and to it; it envelops us in our loves and lives as parents, children, sisters, brothers, husbands, wives, servants, masters, rulers, subjects—the web is seamless and unending.[2] When we talk of virtue, patience, courage, and joy, we talk of what supports it. When we talk of tyranny, lust, and treason, we talk of what destroys it. There is no human action, Shakespeare shows us, that does not affect it and that it does not affect.

Thus, not one of us escapes the Adamic situation. We just decide on what terms we're willing to live with it. We are willing prisoners seeking a joy that survives grief and despair. Or we are unwilling prisoners defiantly railing against unchangeable circumstance. Most times, we're a little of both. Our only hope resides outside us. We are out of control. That's what the Psalmist knows in his heart of hearts and why Jesus gives us the words that I now repeat tremblingly: "Lead us not into temptation, but deliver us from evil." It is also the reason we are encouraged to forgive one another.

---

2. Frye, *King Lear*, 16.

Psalm 5

"My voice shalt thou hear in the morning, O LORD; in the morning will I direct my prayer unto thee, and will look up." (Ps 5:3)

Each morning I wake to myself, a stranger, once more. I'm so insubstantial I'm not sure I remember my own name. Already the day starts as a cliché. It is all so routinized and predictable, I can hardly stand it.

And this is morning! Imagine my vexation at night on finding I am able but reluctant to sleep. For sleep brings dreams—fragments of a failed past—which cause me to wake in a panic, breathless and gasping. I ask, "Where are you at such times, Lord? Is there no peace or protection?" With morning at least there is the comfort of light. But there is also the certainty I am part of someone else's routine dread. Already someone out there has had an imaginary conversation in which he or she has silenced me with witty repartee or the *mot juste*. I know because I've had the same conversation. It's the way of arming myself, while paradoxically remaining totally exposed. A breeze could topple me. Give me your armor, Lord. Don't let me protect myself with vain imaginings. Don't let me reduce people to the predictable responses they know I'll have toward them. Let me see the part of them they would keep secret from me, and let me keep that secret lovingly to myself.

Psalm 6

"Have mercy upon me, O LORD; for I am weak: O LORD, heal me; for my bones are vexed." (Ps 6:2)

I can only assume I'm awake so early for a reason other than to rehearse my anxieties. Maybe I'm supposed to hear your voice in the rain outside. Maybe that is supposed to quieten me for the long (which will turn out to be short) day ahead. How is it Shakespeare described it: "spending again which is already spent"?[1]

As one who is spent, I am waiting for your love to renew the world this morning. But my thoughts are like panic grass, a variety often grown for grain or fodder and whose seed is easily broadcast by the wind. I'm seeking to stay in one place, to find myself rooted to a spot that doesn't swerve in the face of shifting vicissitudes. I'd just as soon it be somewhere where I don't have to take my pulse so frequently or check for the latest symptoms of my demise. It gets old discovering all the new ways I may be dying. So ease my anguish, Lord, for I am weak. My middle-aged bones are vexed. I am weary with my own groaning too. Lord knows, I sound silly to myself at times.

---

1. Ribner and Kittredge, *Complete Works*, 1708.

Psalm 7

"O LORD my God, in thee do I put my trust: save me from all them that persecute me, and deliver me." (Ps 7:1)

Lord, I feel as if I'm sending my children out as sheep among wolves. That, ironically, places me in conspiracy with the wolves. How, I wonder, can I defend my precious children against the indefensible assaults of dull, sad teachers, indifferent administrators, and parents who think nothing of leaving handguns lying around the house as a means of "protecting" their families? Don't they know the enemy is inside the house?

Just the other day, the father of my youngest son's best friend said without thinking (or maybe he'd thought a great deal about it) that it would have been better if so many troublesome, underclass children had not been born. I knew what he meant! For a moment, I even let myself be narcotized by a vision of society in which differences and conflicts no longer existed, in which we could all be comfortable at home with our *own kind*. At least such a society would be safe. I consoled myself for committing mental genocide with the best of intentions.

And that's the problem. Isn't it? We're so damned polite and agreeable that we refuse to be angry for your sake. We'll even agree to commit murder before upsetting people like ourselves. As a result, we haven't made society safe for outcasts, forgetting that our status is always to be outcasts, never to risk being too comfortable with our own kind. Notice my shift from *I* to *we* here, as if a change in pronouns will protect me from the responsibility I refuse to take or the consequences of agreeing with those who would crucify you again for safety's sake.

Psalm 8

"What is man, that thou art mindful of him? and the son of man, that thou visitest him?" (Ps 8:4)

The billboards on my way to work each morning promise me I'm living the good life. Obviously, I need a reminder so I don't forget! Does anyone stop to think about the presence of a sign in the absence of a sign giver? What does such a sign signify?

Sometimes the words of a song or commercial nauseate me. I can't stomach the tired enthusiasms and lavish presumptions that life is only a slogan and nothing more. Can there be a more despairing profession than advertising?

At such times, I want to escape the numbing effect of words and bury my face in the clouds. I look for a sign of your presence in the breasted layers of stratus on the horizon. What do I expect to find there? Only silence and the implacable face of morning. Maybe, I reason, that is a sign in itself. Maybe the creator of all things real doesn't have to rush to offer a message. Maybe that *is* his message. That I am in a position to receive it shows just how mindful he is of me.

Psalm 9

"But the LORD shall endure for ever: he hath prepared his throne for judgment." (Ps 9:7)

It's amazing what an award will do to lift one's spirits. I can be in the doldrums for months—wondering where God is and whether he cares—when all of a sudden, my luck changes. I get what I deserve! In this case, it was a teaching award, one I believed I was long overdue in receiving.

Now my step is lighter. I exude charisma and the sort of dynamic vibration people respond to without knowing why. I'm even willing to share my victory with God. A little mocking voice says, "How generous of you!"

What I secretly know is that I'd have to win the Pulitzer Prize every day in order to feel good even half the time. The only way I can value myself is for the world to value me—to reward me, to shower me with honors. Who can get enough?

Yet Christian theology, in general, and Christ, in particular, make it clear that our joy (if we're to have any joy) must come from something other than the world's view of our accomplishments. Otherwise, our happiness is simply a mania. And the reverse of mania is a free-falling despair into depths one would swear are bottomless.

Who, after all, can say that a person's best efforts won't remain relatively unknown or misinterpreted? As Robert Coles puts it, ". . . such may be the fate of anyone, of even the most talented and sensitive of human beings."[1]

If that's true, shouldn't we take comfort in discovering we're only men and women and that in such discovery hides the possibility of a great joy?

---

1. Coles, "Review," 87.

Psalm 10

"LORD, thou hast heard the desire of the humble: thou wilt prepare their heart, thou wilt cause thine ear to hear." (Ps 10:17)

People don't just do bad things to one another. People deprive each other of good things. Deprivation may be the key to the age as what's good becomes more and more unrecognizable. Yesterday my wife, our son, and I saw a marvelous production of Kafka's *The Trial* performed before an audience of forty. I counted those in attendance. And yet the actors played as if to a full house.

Of those in the audience, however, two-thirds (I estimated) were more than sixty years of age. It occurred to me there might come a time when there would be no audience for Kafka at all. Nobody would see any reason for coming. No one would recall why it is good to examine our contradictions, foibles, absurdities. Maybe no one would see the value, believing despair to be nothing more than a problem already solved by technology.

As regards the human drama, the audience is shrinking who can recognize a good (or bad) thing when it sees it. What is good is what can be sold. What will happen when no one knows why a thing is good? God will play to an empty house, I suppose, "far above, and out of sight." It's almost impossible for people to believe that something good can cease to exist or that they can be deprived of it by choice. Wasn't that Kafka's point in "The Hunger Artist," a story which, if submitted today, would never find a publisher for failure to adhere to a minimalist agenda? Who, after all, wants to believe he or she might be on trial willfully neglecting a goodness that brings forth life? Even if that goodness is no longer recognizable.

Psalm 11

"In the LORD put I my trust: how say ye to my soul, Flee as a bird to your mountain?" (Ps 11:1)

The bobwhite quail is shrinking in large numbers. The reason given is that edges are disappearing. Edges are those shady, wooded areas traditionally left uncultivated by farmers. Now the edges are being bulldozed by the servants of agribusiness who wish to use every inch of available land. The bobwhite no longer has a home—a place to rest. His song is threatened.

Outside my window in the darkness of spring, I hear my friend the bobwhite. I have heard him—only one of him—for two years, I think. His song, a click and two shrill notes, never rests, but continues throughout the night. Comforted, sometimes, I wake to hear him. He lets me know that God is not afraid to sing in the dark. The bobwhite's melody and tempo never alter. He simply stops when morning rises in the east. Usually, he sits in the same place all night. I shift in a hard bed, dreaming of turmoil. Once I dreamed I was whistling and woke to hear the bobwhite. That's when I knew he'd called my soul to the edges. I would miss him if he were gone. He lets me know it's all right to close my eyelids and listen to his call to rest.

Psalm 12

"Who have said, With our tongue will we prevail; our lips are our own: who is lord over us?" (Ps 12:4)

Lord, the world is shrinking, making the strait even narrower for those who refuse to slap you onto bumper stickers or drop you as a cliché in conversation. The alternative to such self-serving and reductionist "praises" of you is not to mention you at all for fear of polluting your name further. Perhaps the best way to be religious in this age is to show no signs of religiosity.

A few days ago, I served as a chaperone for a field trip my son and some of his classmates were taking. As it turned out, several of the dads called at the last minute to say they couldn't make it, leaving a teacher's husband and me as the only men on hand. One of the teachers asked if I'd mind riding in the luggage car rather than on the bus with the kids. I reluctantly agreed. The two women in the van, driver and front seat passenger, were friends, fellow church goers, and professional mothers who resented my presence almost as much as they relished my wife's absence. (She'd wanted to go but figured she'd be unable to room with our son.) It was the last situation that enabled them to generate comparisons of the sort of "godly" (their own word apparently for themselves) sacrifices women make. In the name of preserving society and "returning to morality," these women managed to crucify in conversation: (1) divorced women; (2) working mothers; (3) women in the women's movement; and (4) children (African American) who don't have manners. Within fifteen minutes of conversation between them, corpses lay strewn everywhere. No one, I reasoned, was safe from the assaults of these "women of faith."

In your name, I tried to be civil while registering my protest—even as the common ground was shrinking between us. I pointed out that I knew a good number of divorced and/or working women who were fine and devoted mothers. As for divorce, I suggested the best thing some couples could do was untangle themselves and stop repeating destructive patterns. "Hell," I said, "God never intended for some people to be together in the first place." If uttering the word "hell" didn't do the trick, I went on to note that many of the same people normally opposed to abortion would spare no effort in seeing that "mannerless" underclass children never breathed a breath of God's air or saw the light of day. "Who knows?" I said. "If we could eliminate crime and poverty, abortion on demand might become abortion by demand." The chilly silence that followed lasted only long enough for the driver to insert a tape in the cassette player featuring (I swear to God!) a Christian woman comedian playing to an audience of like-minded Christians somewhere near Atlanta.

Lord, I want to confess that I'd have agreed with anything those women found disagreeable. I'd have supported polygamy, prostitution, or perjury. In short, nothing they said could have redeemed them in my eyes. Fortunately, I don't have to redeem them. They have you for that. I would, however, like to be able to forgive narrow-mindedness without condoning it. I'd especially like to be able to use my words as the broad strokes of a sword sundering a path wide enough for all of us to walk to you in the light.

Psalm 13

"How long shall I take counsel in my soul, having sorrow in my heart daily? How long shall my enemy be exalted over me?" (Ps 13:2)

I am sorrowful today. It seems to be a pattern of late. My wife Linda and I bicker, then criticize each other, then feel remorse and sadness at having done so. This is a hard time for us. During the past three years, the volume of stress we've experienced has increased exponentially. Death, health problems, changes at work—all have contributed to our sense of helplessness. Before, we always seemed to be able to help one another. Now we don't seem to be able to help ourselves, let alone each other. The despair we feel is palpable.

With the Lord's help, we will weather this storm and find safe haven. In the meantime, we both need the patience, compassion, and faith required to endure a turbulent passage, the swells and eddies that test a person to the limits. For my part, I need to die daily to the old self that so often proves an enemy to my true self, the as-yet-to-be discovered being who can, with conviction, "rejoice in thy salvation." Until that I will ask God to remember me in my sorrow and to help me confront the enemies of anger, impatience, and self-pity that would "prevail against" me without his merciful intervention.

Psalm 14

"The fool hath said in his heart, there is no God. They are corrupt, they have done abominable works, there is none that doeth good."
(Ps 14:1)

Most days I'm confronted by the fact that life is a tragedy. After all, we leave home each day with insufficient knowledge but are required to behave as if we're omniscient. We're buffeted by forces we can see and ones we can't. Believing we're acting consciously, we're too often victimized by unconscious impulses, lusts, fears, fantasies, and death wishes of every variety. It's a perilous proposition—living most days.

Yet, occasionally I'm reminded that bleak appearances belie a more comic reality. After all, Christianity makes a claim for redemption. In that sense, then, it is a comic religion in which, no matter what terrors we encounter on the landscape of life, there is always a guarantee of living happily ever after. Perhaps it is a deep and intuitive sense of this reality that explains our fascination with myths, fairy tales, and fantasy literature.

Not so with everyone, however. Just today a friend forwarded me an article from the *London Telegraph* entitled "Harry Potter fails to cast spell over Richard Dawkins." Author of *The Selfish Gene* and arguably the world's more famous atheist, Dawkins plans to discover "whether tales of witchcraft and wizardry have a negative effect on children." Operating from a series of foregone conclusions, Dawkins is "stepping down from his post at Oxford University to write a book aimed at youngsters in which he will warn them against believing in 'anti-scientific' fairytales." "I haven't read Harry Potter," Dawkins admits.[1] Of course, he doesn't have to. As if by some magical act of divining, Dawkins knows what he would find in the Potter series without having to read a single page.

---

1. Dawkins, "Harry Potter Fails," 14.

Psalm 14

I met Dawkins last year at Oxford when I delivered a paper at the Oxford Round Table positing that the language of spirituality was mythic, fatalistic, and paradoxical, by necessity. Arriving late for our session, Dawkins gave the air of someone too busy to stay in one place very long and too distracted to give proper attention to anyone else's ideas. If I had an astrological chip on my shoulder (Dawkins would scoff at such an ancient but unscientific form of knowledge!), I might describe Dawkins as a typical Aries: someone who is impulsive, acting first, asking questions or having doubts later. Ironically, people who dabble in astrology describe people born under the sign of Aries as the most "naïve and childlike of individuals in the Zodiac. They are children at heart and the world is always a magical place for them." What better word than *naïve* to describe the contradictory tendency to "demolish" mythical thinking while, in the same breath declaring, as Dawkins does, "I don't know what to think about magic and fairy tales"?[2] Nor what better evidence demonstrating that humans are anything but rational creatures?

It consoles me to know that we are all cosmic clowns, characterized by folly, foibles, and failures we rarely recognize. Oddly, our status as wise fools peopling a comic universe inspires in me the hope that all is not yet settled and that life, far from being rational, blossoms with mystery and infinite possibility just begging to be discovered by the child in all of us.

2. Dawkins, "Harry Potter Fails," 15.

Psalm 15

"He that backbiteth not with his tongue, nor doeth evil to his neighbor, nor taketh up a reproach against his neighbor." (Ps 15:3)

The impulse to gossip is tantalizing. Part of the enjoyment derives not from spreading lies, but from telling the truth about something—a truth we somehow believe to be concealed from that person. We know about somebody what he or she doesn't know about him or herself. "Have you seen how much weight so and so has gained?" "Lord, where did she get that dress?" "Isn't that his fourth wife?"

My use of the feminine pronoun here is simply for convenience, enabling me to emphasize that men are just as guilty, if not more guilty, of gossiping than women. Neither sex has exclusive rights to the phenomenon.

I am one of the chief offenders. A friend once joked with me at a literary conference, saying, "You try to be good. But you're like a lion in a room full of gazelles. You can't help yourself." He spoke in admiration when describing my quick wit and acid tongue. I felt myself swelling with pride. The well-placed barb, the clever riposte—these are my specialties. After all, who doesn't want to be thought clever?

However, if I think about it long enough, I have to conclude that talking behind someone's back, backbiting, is an appalling form of duplicity. I present myself as one way while being entirely different when out of earshot of the person targeted for assault. There's no other way to describe it than using words as weapons, a sobering thought.

No wonder the Psalmist insinuates that no one can be righteous unless he or she maintains a civil tongue, as my mother used to say. Gossiping, rumor-mongering—these are difficult habits to break once they've been established. However, a bit of forethought suggests that words are energic units; the sort of energy we emit as sound waves can either help or harm those orbiting our proximity. I, for one, have some repenting to do, which means keeping a tight hold on what Anglo-Saxon warriors used to describe as a person's *word haven*.

Psalm 16

"I will bless the Lord, who hath given me counsel: my reins who also instruct me in the night seasons." (Ps 16:7)

I don't know to what the Psalmist was referring exactly in using the phrase "night seasons." It's nonetheless a suggestive term, one aptly fitted to describe some of the shadowy interstices of middle age. Though still in the throes of summer, both my wife and I commented on how the summer solstice signals a hasty retreat toward fall. Just yesterday, July 10, I spent the afternoon soaking up sun on our back deck. At one point, I closed my eyes, listening to a chorus of cicadas tuning up, preparing earlier and earlier each day for night's return: "As night must follow day," as Shakespeare puts it.[1]

I love summer. It's my favorite season. Seeing it go reminds me of the brevity of all of life's seasons—especially at this time in my life. That's why I work hard to notice the goldfinch at my feeder, the Tiger Swallowtail butterfly on a bush outside my window, and the afternoon shadows stretching and yawning on the boards of my back deck. More important is my desire to notice the people I love and the things they love, as well. This morning my wife Linda and I attended Mass where the contemporary music choir sang "Testify to Love," a favorite of ours. One young woman, who has the voice of an angel, sang the chorus solo.

On the way out of church, I said, "Be sure they sing that song at my funeral." Linda responded in kind: "If I go first, make sure they sing it at mine." Those are the kind of instructions we give each other more and more regularly. In the parking lot, it occurred to me that, barring the unlikely event we both die at the same time, one of us will be required to honor the request of the other in some as yet unknown season of the night. At the thought, my heart began to ache at the inconsolable loss we could never

---

1. Ribner and Kittredge, *Complete Works*, 1054.

have imagined on a cold, crisp February afternoon when we spoke our vows, promising to love and honor each other until the inevitable day we would be forced apart.

Psalm 17

"Keep me as the apple of thine eye, hide me under the shadow of thy wings." (Ps 17:8)

According to *Brewer's Dictionary of Phrase and Fable*, the phrase *apple of the eye* refers to the *pupil* because it was anciently supposed to be a round, solid ball like an apple.[1] Figuratively speaking, the term meant anything held extremely dear or much cherished. The phrase is used earlier in the Bible in Deuteronomy 32.10: "He kept him as the apple of his eye."

Truth, of course, comes to us through such images. They aren't simply ornaments but are the substance of our faith, revealing potentially infinite associations and dimensions of meaning. Of course, since ancient times the eye has symbolized an intuitive divination ascribed to seers and prophets. The Masonic origins of US currency find it rich in the imagery of the eye. In another, earlier context in which he describes his rejection of Manichaeism—the belief that all matter and, hence, the body, is intrinsically evil—St. Augustine makes ample use of the eye when recording how hard it is to let go of insubstantial beliefs:

> My heart passionately cried out against all my phantoms, and with this one blow I sought to beat away from the eye of the mind all that unclean troop which buzzed around it. And lo, being scarce put off, in the twinkling of an eye they gathered again thick about me, flew against my face, and beclouded it.[2]

Far from rejecting the human body, Augustine sees it, paradoxically, as an instrument and a gift for experiencing, however imperfectly, the incorruptible, uninjurable, and unchangeable nature of God.

---

1. Brewer, *Dictionary*, 47 (alphabetized in A).
2. Augustine, *Confessions*, 103.

Psalm 17

The apple, too, is charged with mythical and spiritual significance. Although Genesis doesn't specify that the forbidden fruit of the Garden of Eden was the apple, in religious paintings it is almost always depicted as such. Moreover, in ancient mythology, the apple is sacred to Aphrodite, the Greek version of Venus. Closer to our own time and traditions, the mystical isle of Avalon, famed place of eternal rest of Celtic heroes, including King Arthur, literally means *the apple land*.

On a personal note, my grandfather, a farmer, cultivated acres and acres of apple orchards. My favorite of the many varieties was the Winesap apple, a juicy and tart fruit for which I scaled many a tree to pluck just the right one within reach. This experience is one of many reasons I love Robert Frost's poem "After Apple Picking."[3]

The Psalmist clearly understood the powerful coupling of the eye and the apple. Each object is infused with rich associations. When put together, they create a divine alchemy, an expression of concern, consolation, and love for something precious in God's sight. Though wholly unworthy, I'll accept the compliment, happy for a time to be the apple of God's eye.

---

3. Frost, "After Apple Picking."

Psalm 18

"He delivereth me from my enemies." (Ps 18:48)

Since I'm my own worst enemy, I'm asking God to deliver me from myself today. He certainly has his work cut out for him—a lifetime of work, most likely. It's like trying to keep a garden free of weeds. Extricate one, and another, or two, or three pop up in its place. A garden-variety list of my faults includes the following: lusts of all sorts, obsessions of all varieties, and vanities of all descriptions.

I am a child of this world, and, as such, I can never be free of the world's influences. Asking a person to free him or herself from the world's corruption and chaos is like asking prisoners to let themselves out of jail. It can't be done. Someone has to provide the key.

Yesterday I was reading about the Antinomians, an early Christian sect who believed that Christians were not bound to observe the law of God, but could continue in sin that grace might forgive. Martin Luther suggests that we sin bravely and do it in large groups when possible.[1] What a pleasant prospect just to surrender to sin and let come what may! Of course, this prospect was only a momentary fantasy, especially when I recalled that Jesus lived in the same sinful world that I do, nor did he surrender to the notion of just sinning more. As the embodiment of God's warrior, he did not escape our all too human condition, as he well could have done, but stood his ground, enduring the exquisite contradiction between sin and holiness, just as we are called. I won't escape sin today, but I will ask for the strength of one who withstood the test of all that humanity strives to be. Nor was he ever once found lacking!

---

1. Luther, *Letters*, 282.

Psalm 19

"There is no speech or language where their voice is not heard."
(Ps 19:3)

There is no speech or language to describe the love I have for my son Gabriel. He is all sunlight and freckles and a smile as warm as the ocean wind. He is perfect in his happiness, and he enlightens me. For these reasons, Lord, let me be content so that my frustrated ambition does not become his quest—his need to compensate for his father's failures. He loves me and would do what I cannot do for myself. Help him find time. Don't let him get tangled up in my psychological snares or tackle my wounds as his own. I want him to find his joy in you. Help him know that a contented soul is a great gift, sweeter also than honey and the honeycomb. Help him realize he was born to be satisfied, humming your praises in the shower, mouthing silent words that come from you. Yesterday I saw a ruby-throated hummingbird collecting nectar from a flower and thought of my son.

Psalm 20

"Grant thee according to thine own heart, and fulfill all thy counsel."
(Ps 20:4)

The boundaries that once defined sanity and sane relationships among people have all but collapsed. It's almost impossible to say something that doesn't offend someone. Today in one of my classes a woman heard what she wanted to hear (maybe she couldn't hear anything else), taking offense at something she *thought* I'd said. When I repeated my words verbatim, she became even angrier. It was clear she wouldn't be satisfied unless she was right. I was wrong. When I turned to the other students, asking them to verify the account of our conversation, she accused me of manipulating the class and of abusing my authority.

All I was really trying to do was establish the reality of the situation. Now maybe that's impossible when people no longer accept anything as real that doesn't exist outside themselves, or when they cherish their status as victims at the expense of larger possibilities. In any event, teach me, Lord, not to fret over someone else's misplaced anger. Help me not be so resentful at being misunderstood. Don't let me derive my sense of worth from other people so that I secretly hate them when they fail to appreciate me. That's unfair to both them and me.

Psalm 21

"For thou has preventest him with the blessings of goodness." (Ps 21:3)

I am revising my plans for today. In particular, I'm going to keep an eye out for the twin demons of self-pity and self-satisfaction that make me feel more deserving and righteous than God and that prevent me from enjoying the blessing of his goodness. I am going to be "exceeding glad with my countenance." Of course, I don't expect to be aware of all my blessings at once. But I am going to make an effort to pay attention to my breathing, accepting it as a gift rather than a labor.

Or perhaps, I'll pay special attention to someone's face, trying to see something other than what my cynical eyes have taught me to see. After all, don't we teach ourselves to see people's flaws until all we're able to imagine is the "intended evil" against us? Then, Lord, let me see without the aid of my routine vision. Grant me my heart's desire and free me from the habit of despair I've comfortably acquired so as not to have to open new eyes to the world each morning.

Psalm 22

"My God, my God, why has thou forsaken me? why art thou so far from helping me, and from the words of my roaring?" (Ps 22:1)

We all know we're going to die, but no one actually believes it. Time is the subtle thief of youth, causing me to wonder who it is that's staring back at me in the mirror each morning. Last night I dreamed I was dying, victimized by a disease that left me little immunity. "But I don't feel sick," I told the doctors and technicians. "You will soon," they said almost mockingly. I was angry and sad that I'd be leaving my family behind, unable to teach my son how to drive, or show him how to defend himself against the world's constant bullying. I felt helpless. Then I awoke, trembling a little, but remembering it was all a dream. My fears were as a dream from which I woke to hear an early chorus of songbirds. I lay still for a few minutes and finally thought of you, Lord. Why hadn't you come to my aid in the dream? Why did I have to have such a dream in the first place? Why is it that the thought of death is so boggling and incomprehensible? A single breath and the memory of whom I was yesterday are the only evidence I have that I've once again awakened in the land of the living. And what of the time when I have no such evidence, no such memories of the self I've become? Will you be with me then, Lord? Will you remember me then?

Psalm 23

"The Lord is my shepherd; I shall not want." (Ps 23:1)

If I am always right, my prospects are bleak indeed. Being right means being forced to say, "I told you so. God didn't come to my rescue. I could have predicted it." It means never being wrong about the despairing script I write for myself and others. In short, no one can behave out of character. No one can grow or surprise me by changing. I can't surprise myself.

Being wrong, on the other hand, might just mean I don't know how the story will end. I don't have the final word and may have to accept some merciful revisions, ones admitting of unanticipated joys. I may even have to acknowledge that God isn't trying to frustrate me at all but is actually offering alternatives that will eliminate my unquenchable enthusiasm for despair. I can't afford to be right all the time. I've got to be willing to be wrong if God's mercy is to touch and heal me. I've got to be open to the possibility of surprises I accept all too begrudgingly because I didn't think of them first. Finally, I must consider the answer to a question I ask tremblingly: "What if the Lord really is my shepherd?" Then there's absolutely nothing I'm going to lack.

Psalm 24

"Lift up your heads, O ye gates; and be ye lift up, ye everlasting doors; and the King of glory shall come in." (Ps 24:7)

Routine is killing us. We live with so much routine we can scarcely live without it. The sun isn't up yet and already my mind is racing, trying to make all my activities and obligations fit into the single generous gift of a day. "There just isn't enough time," we complain, meaning something other than what we should. What we mean, of course, is that there isn't enough time for all our business=busy-ness. Obviously God wasn't thinking when he gave us only twenty-four hours to get done all we needed to do. He never dreamed we'd be so ambitious, having so many plans of our own. Who has time to "lift up your heads"?

It's true we have little time, which is to say that all the time in the expanding universe is not enough time to "seek God's face," to find him in the hidden dwelling of our heart. Such time is precious indeed. Any time we spend searching for God is like a rare gift given to us for no reason at all. We say, "I have no time," meaning there is no time but now for seeking the God who "dwells therein."

Psalm 25

"O my God, I trust in thee: let me not be ashamed, let not mine enemies triumph over me." (Ps 25:2)

This week I discovered that someone with whom I'd been working on a project wasn't doing her job. Rather than fulfill her obligations, she dumped the project on me, expecting me to rescue her from her own ineptness. I balked. If I have to, I thought, I'll shame her into making good her promise to finish the work. After all, she should feel ashamed.

What I'd forgotten in my rage and overwhelming fatigue was that shame is the last thing a person needs to feel since shame, more than any other human motive, causes us to lie, pretend, and commit to more than we can possibly accomplish. People will kill themselves before having to endure the reproachful finger of shame.

It starts early in childhood. With events so painful we can recall them years later in vivid sensory detail, we learn the unforgettable lesson of shame: that who we are is not enough and that it is, quite literally, possible for us to live without being loved. The resultant despair is something from which few of us recover. Thereafter we are watchful, suspicious, compensating—doing anything for the approval that will keep shame from proving how small and unlovable we really are.

God will not let shame hobble us. He will not let it stunt our growth. He will not let either friends or enemies use our shame to advantage. By sharing our shame on the cross, he refuses to let even death shame us.

Is it any wonder that the Psalmist asks to be delivered from shame: "Let me not be ashamed; for I put my trust in thee." What we can trust is that God has crucified our shame and healed us of its effects. Only human eyes can still see shame. God knows the beauty of his children and smiles.

Psalm 26

"My foot standeth in an even place; In the congregations will I bless the LORD." (Ps 26:12)

I try to stay centered but am not always able. The more peaceful and self-contained I become, the more violent and unpredictable the world becomes. Yesterday, while shopping at Target, I understood why the early church fathers went to the desert to avoid human company. Today the desert is accessible by cell telephone.

Maybe I'm at an awkward age (a phrase I've made for my own amusement). At forty-four, I'm like Charles Dickens's Pip. Many of my Great Expectations have been shattered, which may just be another way of saying my false life has come to an end. The desert is blooming all around me now. There's much cultivating yet to be done.

But the prospect is bewildering, even overwhelming at times. Given my awkward age, I count the days behind me and the ones I might possibly have ahead. The ratio is a little chilling, even if serving to clarify my vision somewhat. St. Paul calls it a race. Maybe he'd reached that awkward age too.

The trick is to run and stay centered at the same time—to let "my foot standeth in an even place." That means resisting the efforts of even well-intentioned people who have no qualms about wasting your time or depleting your energy. Without knowing it, they'll bribe you to take up causes that will steer you off-course, get you lost. That's why it's important to listen to the voice in your dreams, the one that knows the secret of the years behind and the whispering possibility of days remaining. It's a voice that knows its way home, to the habitation where all our days are "wondrous works" in the memory of God.

Psalm 27

"The LORD is my light and my salvation; whom shall I fear? the LORD is the strength of my life; of whom shall I be afraid?" (Ps 27:1)

To the question "Of what should we be afraid?" we can answer, "almost everything." Throughout our culture, fear is so generalized that we think nothing of accepting it or making accommodations to it. Our lives are consciously planned to route us around the objects of our fears. Anxiety and panic, not neurosis and psychosis, are the benchmark disorders of the day. Is it any wonder?

Who of us in our right minds cannot be afraid when told we are being attacked at the cellular level—that our very genes are in rebellion, our immune systems toppled, our defenses under siege. Given these conditions, who of us can offer any confidence to our children, some of whom have been so mutated by fear we can scarcely recognize them? (Are they virtual humans or simply predators? Is there any hope for them—us?)

We are liars in refusing to acknowledge that ours is a culture of fear. Just an hour ago, I overheard two students discussing how to reload an automatic round. "Planning to shoot someone?" I wanted to ask. Nor would their predictable "target practice" have provided a sufficient excuse. After all, why does anyone actually take target practice? We can't afford to be casual any longer.

Doubtless some people will claim that only a fool doesn't take precautions to defend oneself. What this claim ignores is that there is no longer a line of defense for any of us. We're incapable of defending ourselves against chaos, crisis, or collapse. How do we defend ourselves against the air we breathe?

In short, we're helpless. The extent to which we acknowledge our helplessness is the extent to which we can now receive help. We're not in control precisely because God is in control. Does that mean all the predators will go away? Not exactly. What it means is that "When the wicked, even enemies and my foes, came upon me to eat up my flesh, they stumbled and fell." God isn't afraid of predators. He simply feeds them out of his bounty of love.

Psalm 28

"The LORD is my strength and my shield; my heart trusted in him, and I am helped: therefore my heart greatly rejoiceth, and with my song will I praise him." (Ps 28:7)

I've given all I can give. I'm all out of interest, energy, time, and affection. For weeks I've tried to hint that I'm a limited resource—that even I am subject to the laws of thermodynamics. I mistakenly believed that if I just did everything possible to meet everyone else's needs, those needs would subside. People would notice how much I'd been giving and let me rest. That hasn't been the case. My body is one continuous surge of adrenaline. I'm so habituated to looking for opportunities for helping, I don't know any other mode. Now people are peevish because I've reached the end of my endurance. They don't understand why I'm "not myself," why I'm numb, irritable, and inattentive.

It's my fault, really. I let them ask more of me than was humanly possible to give. I let them think I was offering them something less than the gifts of my time and energy—my essence. I forgot that there will always be someone in need of something.

Need is a bottomless pit, and I become "like them that go down into the pit" unless I remember my limitations. While I don't want to ignore anyone's genuine needs, I need to make fine distinctions, recalling that "The Lord is their strength." I can help the Lord, but I can't replace him. There are too many people trying to do that now.

What is the answer? I don't know except to be more direct in saying what I can and cannot do. I do know God has compassion for me as a human being. He knows I need to rest. Even his son became tired and needed rest on his journeys. I can't "clear the boards" before insisting on the time I need to restore myself. The boards will never be clear. The vineyard will always require someone's hands. But I can insist on drawing away from noisy requests that never end. I can insist on claiming the cornerstone of peace the busy builders reject.

Psalm 29

"The voice of the LORD is upon the waters: the God of glory thundereth: the LORD is upon many waters." (Ps 29:3)

My pulse is normal, my breathing easy. Such peace can only come from without. I certainly didn't manufacture it. Just to sit and hear noise beyond the door is a luxury. It is interesting how a few moments' stillness will open a window to memories and impressions—the once hopeful and ever-changing sky of childhood. For me the scene is one of a stream bickering at mid-morning in the woods near the house where I grew up. Living in a semi-rural area without brothers or sisters, I was often my own playmate, creating characters who played with me and served as allies and foils in the continuous heroic adventure that was childhood. I recall singing songs with words I'd made up. No one heard me. I was alone without being the least bit lonely.

On that day in memory, I bent over the shallow running stream and watched my young face smile, the trembling reflection of a stranger with whom I'd had only eight years to become acquainted. I liked the boy I saw there but didn't know him very well, didn't even know what he was. Listening to the trill of my own falsetto voice, I became aware that all time existed in me but that I was outside of time too. I was both the self I was becoming, but something else, something uncreated that could watch me being created. At that instant, I knew God had entered my awareness. Instinctively, I looked up to see giant oaks and hickories, fluttering, creating the dappled light of morning. I kept singing.

Whenever I think of childhood, I naturally think of water. What child isn't drawn to a stream? Maybe the reason is found in the words of the Psalmist: "The voice of the Lord is upon the waters: the God of glory thundereth: the Lord is upon many waters." Is it a coincidence that when I have the luxury of losing track of time, I return to my stream, to the place where all of me can be found singing? And what of the boy staring back from the trembling water. Where did he go?

Psalm 30

"Thou hast turned for me my mourning into dancing: thou hast put off my sackcloth and girded me with gladness." (Ps 30:11)

A week or so ago, I read an article on longevity. The article included a checklist of activities that detract from one's lifespan (e.g., smoking, drinking, stress on the job, high blood pressure). Interestingly enough, despair and self-pity were nowhere on the list. Neither were the seven deadly sins, which in our time have been refined into vices. From the list anyone could predict life expectancy. How comforting that we have been given permission to live as long as possible. By their count, I could make it thirty years more. God forbid that God should decide otherwise.

I must confess I'm not as confident as the actuarial experts. Also, I must confess to having wasted much of the precious life I've been given. That may not be an unforgiveable sin, but it probably comes close. I mean that literally. What I'm beginning to realize is that regret itself is just one more obstacle to living fully. I'm worrying about what I haven't accomplished—the books I haven't written, the fame I haven't acquired. All I succeed in doing is aborting the life I've been given at this moment, which is not a moment at all. What if we really believed, as Tolstoy did, that the kingdom of God is within us and that time is not a matter of duration, but of transformation? Time is, therefore, a gift, an opportunity for letting me participate in eternity as long as I don't let despair and the fear of death keep me from believing time to be a limited quantity. That's especially important when so much contrary evidence stares back at me in the mirror each morning. It's not as if we don't "age" or participate in the human condition that counts us all worthy of dying sooner or later. But our faith should be an affront to such appearance. Our faith tells us that even in the act of dying, we do not die. We embrace all time.

When I was a small child (admittedly a strange one), I often felt my world to be a terrifying place. And so I envisioned the inside of my body as a series of the compartments or rooms where everyone I loved could live safely. Maybe I knew even then that the kingdom of God's love was inside me—timeless and intact. I hope so.

Now I ask God's mercy each day for all the members of my family and for people I do not know—people as countless, it seems, as grains of sand on a beach. I ask for God to keep us safe within the kingdom of his body where we can love each other for eternity, praying to God that eternity is not simply an endless duration of time. That would be the definition of hell. Instead, I pray that eternity is the starting point where love multiplies itself infinitely. After all, we take God's body into us that we may become a part of God's body. In doing so, we share immortality, defeating natural process and its attendant vice of despair. We also make actuarial predictions the butt of a cosmic joke. For in the words of the Psalmist, we have turned "mourning into dancing" and will "not be silent" so happy are we to love "forever."

Psalm 31

"For I've heard the slander of many: fear was on every side: while they took counsel together against me, they devised to take away my life."
(Ps 31:13)

The way you give energy to the demons of despair is to recall all the insults and hurts you've received for as long as you can remember. If possible, go back to childhood when such injuries were new and only beginning to assume mythological proportions. Find the wound of greatest important, the one that continues to shame you, the one that is the site of your greatest anguish. That's where the demons have free access to your body and soul. That's where the demons rise up to whisper "lying vanities" and "the slander of many."

I've known demons to cause people to give up on themselves. I've known demons to create conditions that resulted in cirrhosis, cancer, and suicide. I've known intelligent, sensitive, and kind people who've become casualties to forces they could not identify but which devised to take away their lives. In short, I believe, demons are every bit as real as the conditions they cause. Nor does saying they're simply psychological manifestations (i.e., root=festation) explain their origin.

They know us—sometimes better than we know ourselves. Therein lies their power. They convince us there is only one story worth listening to—theirs. And it is a story of our worthlessness as children, as parents, as workers in the vineyard of our professions. Our response to this overriding sense of worthlessness is a rage that demons use to their advantage, convincing us not to let anyone near the wound. As long as we go along with their version of things and accept our unworthiness as a natural state of affairs, the demons are normally quiet. After all, we're subdued. But let someone compliment us or let us succeed in a way recognized by others and the demons will be all too happy to remind us of our unworthiness. Think about it: Are we unhappiest when we fail or when we succeed? Is there ever enough success to make us feel we have escaped the hold the demons have on us. Do we ever get to the point where we refuse to listen to "the strife of tongues" urging us to reject our status as the children of God? And what of the phrase "children of God"? Isn't that proof of our worth? To God, our worth is never an issue. It is an inviolable certainty.

So, Lord, "let the lying lips be put to silence, which speak grievous things proudly and contemptuous against us." Send your angels to guard the site of our woundedness until you can heal a "life(time) spent with grief and years of sighing." Give us courage to reject the voices that diminish us, making so much emotional noise we can scarcely hear you at times. Let our heads be quiet and our hearts strong enough to survive all we've endured. Finally, let us recall how worthy we must really be if so many voices are trying to convince us otherwise.

Psalm 32

"Blessed is he whose transgression is forgiven, whose sin is covered."
(Ps 32:1)

Just yesterday my wife Linda was telling me about an agency she'd visited where the employees are advocates for infants with birth defects. The babies this agency serves are born with some of the most appalling deformities and hopeless conditions imaginable. In an age when so much value is attached to physical perfection, these children remind us that we live in an imperfect world. They are a humble affront to all our pretensions and all our efforts to forget our fragile human condition. In a sense, these children have made the ultimate sacrifice by showing us that not even the innocent escape the ravages of sin.

Our tragedy is that we inherit and pass on the genetic consequences of our sinfulness. It is sin that all too often connects us with generations that came before us and with those to come. It is this sympathetic link that unites past and future through the conduit of our present experience. As if the genetic expression of sinfulness weren't enough, we are born to families whose dysfunctional patterns are sometimes repeated for generations. In his book *The House of Percy*, Bertram Wyatt-Brown discusses the pattern of suicide found in one of the South's most illustrious literary families—a family including such luminaries as William Alexander Percy and Walker Percy, arguably the most important American novelist since Faulkner. As Wyatt-Brown points out, the Percys killed themselves with a fair degree of regularity, giving rise to the somewhat romantic notion that the family was genetically predisposed to depression and suicide.[1] Maybe. But to impute sadness and despair to biological causes is to ignore a more pressing and ominous reality: negative feelings and inadequate strategies for

---

1. Wyatt-Brown, *House of Percy*, 3–361.

adjustment are learned. Children imitate what parents model for them. What we pass on to our children are the habits of feeling we acquired from our own parents.

Yesterday, I was jogging when it suddenly occurred to me that everything I did in a given day laid the groundwork for what future generations—my children's children and their children, too—would or would not be able to do at that instant, making choices that would result in unforeseeable consequences. Hence the need to be as aware as possible of my own blind spots, inadequacies, imperfections. I prayed for the Lord to give me knowledge of my sins so I wouldn't pass on the consequences of those sins to the as-yet unborn. I asked God to enter the natural process in order to release me from the generational shackles that enslave me and my children. That God can tear up the sinful works of time is a mystery I cannot fully comprehend. Nevertheless, it is a mystery I'm willing to accept on faith in the face of so much suffering.

Psalm 33

"Let all the earth fear the LORD: let all the inhabitants of the world stand in awe of him." (Ps 33:8)

I'm beginning to suspect that some of the alarms and shocks I've been experiencing can be attributed to my "rebirth" here in middle age. There is some truth to the idea that middle age offers an opportunity for a new life. In men, the period of middle life has been compared to adolescence and more and more I notice men my age driving the red sports cars they were unable to own in their teens or shooting basketball with knee braces they didn't used to require. But I think the analogy stops there. The fact is that middle-aged men are far more bewildered than their adolescent counterparts. Adolescent males are almost never bewildered. They know exactly what they want—to grow up.

Most middle-aged men aren't certain about anything. A better analogy would probably compare the middle years to infancy. That's because babies are often bewildered. Having been something else or perhaps nothing but a memory waiting to happen, babies must grow accustomed to being human. So mysterious are they to themselves at first! They must learn to take themselves for granted. They must lose some sense of the infinite act of discovering themselves as nothing like anything they would have imagined. In my early twenties, I had a conversation with my father who was in his fifties. He said, "Sometimes I'm just driving down the road and start wondering, 'Who am I and what am I here for?' Then I'll just stare at my hand. Do you know what I mean?" I pretended or perhaps even thought I did. The truth is that I had to drive the road a while longer to get to the place where my father's experience coincided (or maybe *collided* is a better word) with my own. As with most births, mine finds me new to whatever it is I'm becoming. Despite all my efforts to keep my body alive and young (and I seem to be doing a pretty good job), my outward husk of a body will eventually die, just as my father's did. However, there are compensations in aging, in being reborn. One is not taking for granted the newness that infuses life with a sense of awe. Such makes watching the twinkle in my wife's eye or the shape of my son's growing legs an act of meditation like no other. It is their otherness in which I find unspeakable mystery and the presence of God that enables me to rejoice.

Psalm 34

"What man is he that desireth life, and loveth many days, that he may see good?" (Ps 34:12)

My son Gabriel will be twelve this week. He's excited—not because he's going to be twelve but because he's going to have a birthday. He loves birthdays. My son is still a little boy, thank God.

Last night I'd almost drifted off to sleep when I snapped awake in panic. I couldn't remember some features of his babyhood I desperately wanted to remember. I was also overwhelmed by the smothering sensation that there was so little time and still so much I needed to do for him to make his childhood one capable of sustaining him. I want him to recall his time with his mother and me as an experience of great joy and as a deep well of love from which he can drink all his days. When we had him, we had only the vaguest sense we would one day be giving him up to adulthood. Now the clock ticks—no, thunders, in my ears. And so I woke last night in fear and trembling, hoping we'd done all we'd needed to at this point and praying for time to do what we still needed to do.

We named him after the angel Gabriel, meaning "God is my strength." It was the first blessing we bestowed upon him and the first prayer we offered on his behalf. He was our hand-held miracle, and he will never know how deliriously we have loved him. Now it is my—our—job to see that he does not lack all the love that is his birthright as a child of God but given to us in sacred trust. Is it any wonder I panic and lose sleep and wait for the opportunity a new morning offers? The Psalmist understood perfectly when he said, "What man is he that desireth life, and love the many days, that he may see Good?" Lord, grant us many days of love together. Accept my gratitude for the days we've been given. And keep my son's blue eyes safe for seeing you forever.

Psalm 35

"False witnesses did rise up; they laid to my charge things that I knew not." (Ps 35:11)

Through no fault of my own, there are people I will inevitably disappoint. No amount of time I spend with them will be enough. No amount of encouragement or reassurance will satisfy them. I am doomed to fail them because, unconsciously or otherwise, they have created the conditions whereby I can't do anything else. Such a situation only creates frustration and hard feelings for everyone involved. People become enemies without knowing why.

I believe I know why. People who are chronically disappointed are victims of their own unworthiness. In proving that other people disappoint them, they actually prove that they're worthy of being disappointed. Put another way: if you fail me, it must be because I deserve to be failed. Because no one can or should be required to feel such failure, the alternative is to offer a defense of the self by blaming someone else—by projecting the failure one feels onto someone in the unenviable position of not being able to fulfill impossible needs.

The lesson here is that people rarely fail us as much as we think. If you find yourself disagreeing with the previous statement or becoming angry at my failure to understand your particular anguish, then you are the owner of an unacknowledged rage that will of necessity seek to justify itself. Unfortunately, such justification usually occurs at someone else's expense, someone who does not deserve the emotional upheaval that occurs when "false witnesses did rise up; they laid to my charge things that I knew not. They rewarded me evil for good to the spoiling of my soul."

Psalm 36

"Let not the foot of pride come against me, and let not the hand of the wicked remove me." (Ps 36:11)

Why does my mind's eye return to the playground of my childhood? Is it because that's where I first learned the art of making friends and enemies, of making the sacred-profane discovery of qualities both attractive and repugnant to me? In my primitive, often irrational alliances, I began to locate a core of characteristics that formed the vision of the person I wanted to be. Later, I would find variations of that person in literature, represented, archetypically by such characters as Robin Hood, King Arthur, the avenging Lancelot, and Shane. Often my heroes brooded over their difficulties. They displayed doubts. But I could count on them in the end to be heroic, fierce, loyal, vigilant, tough, intelligent, and protective of the weak. They worked hard not to disappoint themselves or other people. I tried to follow their example.

A friend of mine tells a story his brother told him. His brother recalled how a group of fifth grade boys were once picking on a third grader. Although only a fourth grader myself, I came to the younger boy's rescue by climbing a fence and offering to fight the gang of fifth graders (*gang* didn't carry such dangerous connotations then). I can still taste the copper fear in my mouth. But I recall my resolve too. As hopelessly sentimental as is that story, I realize its events with pride. I wish I could say I've always been that brave. I wish I could say I hadn't grown so polite that I sometimes ignore or excuse bullying now. For what I know is that we do not fool ourselves as children. We are both our best and worst selves. We are also our most real.

Never let it be said I didn't know my enemies. I had enough respect for them to recognize them as real. An adult will lie, saying that there are no enemies, only misunderstandings. Unfortunately, such an attitude reflects not only the adult's sense of spiritual superiority, but his status as a survivor with amnesia. Children, on the other hand, can't afford to be so foolish.

With that in mind, we should be careful not to forget the time when our enemies were real, giving us opportunity to renounce them or grow up like them. Nor can we afford to see people for other than who they sometimes really are. Where is the possibility of salvation in doing otherwise? A nun once told me that all children needed to do was "talk nice" to one another. Sometimes that's the last thing children need to do. Sometimes they just need to climb the fence, point a finger at the enemy, and say *stop*. That someone might be afraid of doing that is probably all the evidence required that it needs doing.

Psalm 37

"The righteous shall inherit the land, and dwell therein forever."
(Ps 37:29)

Imagine arriving at the end of your life and discovering you were supposed to have done something else, been someone different. Can you imagine the Lord saying, "You were to have been a great saint like Mother Teresa. Your destiny was to transform the world in my name. Instead, you became choked and troubled with the care of this world, feeling smaller than you should. Now what do you have to show for the gifts I've given you?" It is a sobering prospect, a chilling form of judgment. Yet even our prayers are full of fear and concern and a desire to shrink from the large place God has asked us to occupy and which is our birthright by inheritance: "The righteous shall inherit the land and dwell therein forever."

What reasons can we offer when all we have to offer are excuses? Can we say we were simply victims of the times in which we lived? I don't think so. Do we place our faith in the currents of the day and hope, by some miracle, they don't sweep us away? Everywhere we look is a subtle message telling us we'd better go along with the status quo or we'll be left out, forgotten in the new technological economy that treats time as something it owns. And what of the movers and shakers in this new economy? Don't they threaten to abandon us, to count as inconsequential all those who fail to affirm their vision of reality, which is, to say, unreality? We must teach our children to be suspicious of anyone who says, "I have something you can't live without. Go along with me and I'll see you're taken care of. Fail to do so and you'll be left behind—a nobody exiled on an increasingly shrinking island." We must teach our children that time does not belong to such people and that God provides for his exiles. Better to stay on the island with God than to swim in the mainstream where sharks are a fixture on the subterranean landscape. To shift the metaphor a bit: to be accepted in the mainstream may be ultimately to drown there. Our meditation and our children's meditation should be on the timeless promise of God's love that is given freely and is never withheld, only rejected: "Trust in the Lord, and do good; so shalt thou dwell in the land and verily thou shalt be fed."

Psalm 38

"They also that seek after my life lay snares for me: and they that seek my hurt speak mischievous things, and imagine deceits all the day long." (Ps 38:12)

Anxiety isn't just psychological in origin. It has its roots in the unspeakably frightening but unavoidable spiritual dilemma we all face. Almost everywhere I look these days, there is evidence that people are desperate to live forever. The media promise new cures and tantalizing combination of herbs and anti-aging formulas that none of us, paradoxically, can live without.

Our current mania to live youthfully and forever is symptomatic of a very old struggle to cheat death. God may not be real to us, but death certainly is real. We worship death; we give him thanks when he stays away. Like the pagans of old, we simultaneously placate and avoid. All of this idolatry exists because we believe our death more real than our lives. We want to live forever, not because we revere and appreciate the precious gift of life, but because we suspect, deep down, we haven't learned to live at all. In fact, for most people in the industrialized world, life is tedious business. But what, after all, is the alternative?

Anyone who does not experience anxiety in the face of this genuine spiritual crisis is already dead, which is why anxiety affords an opportunity to wake up to ourselves as we really are. No wonder the Psalmist worries that God may be rebuking him. God will not let us "imagine deceits all day long." But we have to listen, listen to the disturbing voice that will not let us sleep nights, the one that makes us tremble with fear at the prospect of dying out of life. And what if we don't know how to live? What if we've utterly forgotten? Then we ask God to do what we can't do for ourselves: to remove death by placing himself on the altar of our despair.

Psalm 39

"LORD, make me to know mine end, and the measure of my days, what it is: that I may know how frail I am." (Ps 39:4)

Try to imagine all the people who've died anonymously. The thought is staggering. The other day I was reading a book about the Civil War and came across a photograph taken of soldiers laid out for burial. No one recalls a one of them now. Eventually no one will remember any of us either. Who, after he or she is dead, is known beyond a small circle of family, friends, and acquaintances who themselves will one day die? The lives we lived and took so seriously will be utterly forgotten by people who, in the natural course of time, will never know we existed.

Very few people survive the test of memory that history affords. And there is no guarantee that the people and deeds we deem worth remembering will be ones valued and recalled by future generations. Those people may have new criteria. In a real sense, our legacy to them depends on us and what we, as anonymous benefactors, are urgent to teach, to pass on to our anonymous beneficiaries. Thus, although our failures will not be known to us, they will be seen, felt, and analyzed by our anonymous spiritual children.

We live to be forgotten, a fact that awaits us. That's why it's important to pray that we do God's will now. Soon we will be nameless once more, waiting for the name God gives us. The one by which we have been known for eternity, the one by which we have been called to life in him. We live only to the extent we are remembered—by God.

Psalm 40

"But I am poor and needy; yet the LORD thinketh upon me: thou art my help and my deliverer; make no tarrying, O my God." (Ps 40:17)

Life will not be denied. It waits patiently and finds a way. That is God's promise. At times I wonder if anyone ever stops to consider why, with all our advanced knowledge and technological means and compulsory sexual education, girls continue to become pregnant out of wedlock at an alarming rate. At least, it's alarming to people who wonder why these girls don't know any better. Most do, for all the reasons listed above. But something else is operating here, I think. And that is the ability of life to circumvent all our good intentions and technological solutions to the "problem" of pregnancy. How many times have we heard the well-intentioned, "compassionate" argument for abortion on the grounds that the last thing the world needs is another unwanted child? That begs a crucial question: unwanted by whom? How have we managed to forget that it is God, not we, who authors life and who is the father of all his children?

    Amazing are the number of times in the Bible when life seems thwarted, frustrated, impossible to conceive. Yet, as in the case of Sarah, who believed herself too old to bear a child, God finds a way, even offering reassurance: "Is anything too hard for the Lord?"[1] No, life, which is to say the Lord, will not be denied. If the more privileged and technologically sophisticated among us will not answer the call to life, then God will simply turn to the humble, the scorned, and the despised—just as he always has. Is it any wonder then that the poor and uneducated continue to confound us by bearing the fruit of souls God has destined for life? We have made it impossible for such people to do otherwise. Still, God bestows upon them the blessings of life we reject and keeps in mind those whom we all too

---

1. Gen 18:14.

easily forget: "But I am poor and needy; yet the Lord thinketh upon me: thou art my help and my deliverer; make no tarrying, O my God."

Psalm 41

"The LORD will strengthen him upon the bed of languishing: thou wilt make all his bed in his sickness." (Ps 41:3)

It is 4 a.m. —the witching hour. A little while ago I woke from a dream, the details evaporated now, in which I was experiencing anxiety about something or other I couldn't control. I can't remember the dream, though it ended with my punting a football and being surprised by the force of my kick. I suppose, symbolically and psychologically, I was punting whatever problem I couldn't solve. Afterwards I lay in the "bed of languishing," as the Psalmist calls it, trying unsuccessfully to return to sleep. Trying to sleep is a contradiction, so I decided to get up and confront the demons that so earnestly seek my attentions, "mine enemies" of doubt and hopelessness that never tire of asking: "When shall we die, and his name perish?" Are other people awakened by such whispers? Why is it I secretly believe that if I sleep too much, I'll die? Such is the metaphor of my life, it seems, and I would not be surprised if the enemies I've mentioned are really my friends in disguise, awakening me to the fear and trembling of my authentic condition, which is that I'm living inauthentically. Sometimes it seems people my age have made peace with life in a way I haven't done yet. Or perhaps I'm travelling backwards on my spiritual journey, a frustrating thought and one I was forced to consider yesterday on encountering two people from my not-so-distant, but irretrievable, past.

The first was a woman at church whose name I couldn't recall at first, but who'd been a student of mine, she informed me, some eighteen years ago. "I would have recognized you anywhere," she remarked. "You haven't changed a bit." I laughed, thanked her for the intended compliment, apologizing for whatever sort of college instructor I must have been at twenty-six. To tell the truth, I may have been better in some ways that I am now. I was certainly more sure of myself, more confident that I was responding to a call. Of course, uncertainty and doubt can be indicators of maturity too, of waning illusion. At least, I hope so. But I couldn't help wondering where the time had gone and if I'd indeed changed for the better.

My second encounter came with a phone call. As before, the caller was a former student, though a man a few years older than I. He'd recently received a PhD in philosophy and was applying for a job at the college where I teach. We discussed the lack of interest people have in the humanistic disciplines these days and how science and technology are the princes of the age. He teasingly complained that his vocation is philosophy and that it was my fault. "You conned me into believing this was a noble profession," he said, his voice showing a slightly exposed razor's edge of seriousness now. "You should have gone into something practical," I responded, "like English." For all our banter, there was a genuine doubt about the paths we'd chosen.

Fortunately, being awake at the witch's hour gives the mind a chance to range freely over the previous day's mysteries, often disguised as habits to be acquired or routines to be learned. In particular, I was helping my son yesterday afternoon with a martial arts combination of strikes, commenting on the importance of proper technique. "There'll come a time in your life," I said, "—and I'm not just talking about martial arts—when you'll panic and doubt your technique. Other people will be doing things you'll think you've never seen before, and they'll try to persuade you to do what they're doing. They'll spare no effort, implying that what you know is of no value. At that point, dig in. Rely on your technique, on the habits that you've already learned and that will not fail you because you took no shortcut acquiring them. In that instant, your fear will dissolve because you will be real enough to stand the test and to call down God's help for one he'll recognize as having worked in the dark to weave motion of light you could never have anticipated."

Psalm 42

"Deep calleth unto deep at the noise of thy waterspouts: all thy waves and thy billows are gone over me." (Ps 42:7)

Outside there is a lull in the crickets' enthusiasm as autumn is almost on us. My wife Linda says she welcomes fall because life returns to her in that season. By contrast, I am summer's advocate, mourning its brevity and groaning like a child forced to leave the playground and return to class. Yesterday I was walking near the lake and spotted some purple pokeweed with even more purple berries. As children, my pals and I would crush the berries, making what we called Indian dye out of them. What we made, of course, was a mess.

Many are the mornings I wake and wonder about my childhood companions. At times, I even say a prayer for them, hoping the mystery of their lives has deepened into "joy and praise" for all they've become in the years since we first played. After all, by what act of grace were we brought together in the first place, and what did we learn by being children together? It is a mystery worth contemplating, though I suspect I'll never reach the bottom of it since "deep calleth unto deep," as the Psalmist says. I may have to be content to recall the melancholy droning of crickets outside the window of a room where I once slept.

Sometimes I think I'm the only fool in existence. No one else, it seems, bothers much about time. Almost everyone I know accepts the passing of the seasons without a murmur. Then I recall how St. Augustine reminds us that even during a brief conversation, our hair continues to grow, though never so suddenly that we need a barber straightaway.[1] In this way, our existence fades away. We pass on.

---

1. Augustine, *Confessions*, 130.

Once, at about age eight, I climbed up into a swing set and watched the rim of a furious sun disappear behind the silhouette of distant hills. It was the first time in my life I felt carried beyond myself and the place where I happened to be sitting. It was also the first time I understood that I could be in two places at once, grieving for one without wanting to leave the other.

Psalm 43

"Then I will go unto the altar of God, unto God my exceeding joy: yea, upon the harp will I praise thee, O God, my God." (Ps 43:4)

In his book *Thoughts on Solitude*, Thomas Merton offers the following observation:

> The fear which is the first step to wisdom is the fear of being untrue to God and to ourselves. It is the fear that we have lied to ourselves, that we have thrown down our lives at the feet of a false god.[1]

If Merton is correct (and I have no reason to believe he isn't), then I will embrace my fear as a friend rather than try to subdue it as an enemy. What I fear most, I've concluded, is that I have spent my life failing to fulfill my vocation as a *human being*. Have I really answered God's call? When was the last time I listened to what he had to say to me? Or do I simply carry on my routine and assume I know what he has in store? *I know best what God wants me to do.* Has a more paradoxical statement ever been uttered?

Now I'm forced to confront the possibility that even when I thought I was doing God's will, I wasn't. As Merton says, "Every man is a liar for every man is a sinner."[2] What I have to acknowledge is that I've been lying to myself, exalting my goodness and worshipping the shaky image, the self-conscious and bloated me I've created to compete with God. Is it any wonder God disappoints me or that I'm ashamed of him at times? He fails to do my bidding. He doesn't conform to my expectations. He refuses to consider my plans. Doesn't he know how much I do for him?

God is truth and, as such, is beyond bribery. That is both good and bad news. How comforting Merton understood that he realized the Devil

---

1. Merton, *Thoughts*, 73.
2. Merton, *Thoughts*, 73.

might actually have the last laugh but for a fear that awakens us to our true selves. If fear is the beginning of wisdom, then I thank God for letting me be afraid. What I've been calling my enemy, I'm beginning to see in a different light.

Psalm 44

"For I will not trust in my bow, neither shall my sword save me."
(Ps 44:6)

Sometimes I'm able to recognize my family's enemies and give a name to them. For my wife Linda, it's the specter of downsizing, an accepted, even encouraged form of corporate murder that wrecks lives and sends families spiraling for years. Such decisions are based on the need of people to feel powerful, justified, and, above all, smugly practical. If in America, money is more important than death, as one writer has noted, then what are the reasons for living? Or, as a friend of mine wrote me last week asking: "Why is it that fools are made administrators time and again? Is there some form they fill out ascertaining they lack reasoning skills, empathy, and wisdom?"

As for my wife, I know of no one who takes Christ's image more lovingly into the workplace. Nor do I know anyone who fights harder to protect the people she supervises, supports, counsels, and loves. Above her and her colleagues often looms the shadow of an ax, the sharp edge of which she has deflected time and time again with enormous expenditures of energy, creativity, and resourcefulness. It is no accident she has survived insensitivity, crassness, rumors, character attacks, and orchestrated efforts to dismantle the solid foundation of work it has taken years to complete.

If my wife's enemy thrives by making her wonder, doubt, and worry, my twelve-year-old son Gabriel's nemesis survives by offering two contradictory images, each posing as the other. Often, Gabriel's enemy doesn't know the contradiction it offers, the schizophrenic expectation it imposes on children who are striving for unity of spirit. It simply presents a message: Love like an angel but compete like hell. Nowhere is this message more evident than in the Catholic school he attends. There my son learns that we are all one as long as none of us falls through the cracks. It is an attitude held by a number of parents who wait for their children in the parking lot each afternoon and who, for some reason, believe they have plenty of economic incentive for ignoring those even slightly less fortunate than they. In my more cynical moments, I refer to them as the "Ute tribe," named in honor of the sport utility vehicles they own as status symbols. Many of the same people attend Mass where they hear how Christ ministered to the poor. I can only assume they believe he was a liar.

My son knows better. He understands that unbridled, showy competition—competition that tramples the competitor into the dust—is at odds with Christ's teachings. He even opts at times to lose rather than pretend that winning under such circumstances is acceptable. Although he is, for the most part, as gentle as a dove, my son is as wise as a serpent when it comes to detecting self-justifying behaviors. Contradiction creates bitterness, but my son sings when he thinks no one is listening.

My own song is bittersweet, given that my enemy lurks on the cusp of disappointment and hope. My family is my Israel. I work for them, pray for them, and would if necessary, I hope, die for them. I would offer them a perfect world if I could. Unfortunately, I cannot. The extent to which I am sometimes helpless to help them, my students, and my friends is a source of great despair to me. Knowing this, my enemy is quick to take advantage of my weakness, whispering in my ear: "It's no use. You'll never achieve the results you want. You're a fool to try."

But the enemy has overplayed his hand. He has only pointed out the obvious: where I fail, God is capable of succeeding. In fact, it is only my failure that permits God to enter the sphere of my life, transforming dismal results into unimagined possibilities. How different does failure appear in the light of God's willingness to redeem "us for kindness's sake." How different our lives become when we shout "Arise! Help us," and he does.

Psalm 45

"My tongue is the pen of a ready writer." (Ps 45.1)

I teach writing, so this verse has special appeal to me. I can't remember a time when I didn't write. Even now I'm preparing to go on vacation where I'll spend each morning, before anyone else rises, penning a lecture I'm to give at my college in the fall on the dangers of teaching-machine education—the indiscriminate use of stimulus-response modules and distance delivery systems. These are the inventions of edu-business corporations and thus have more to do with profit than with teaching and learning of the sort that promises a person the possibility of a contemplative life.

A student of mine wrote me a note the other day in response to a handwritten letter I'd sent her. She wondered why anyone would prefer "the dull fonts of a lifeless machine" to the unique expressions of calligraphy:

> My soul, seemingly apart from this time and place, grieves handwritten correspondence, now called lost art. Doesn't anyone miss the silken curves of sibilant-S and the strong downward strokes of a pen fitting perfectly in one's hand, telling every secret, revealing unspoken hope?

Her own soul's yearning is beautifully expressed here in shapes bearing the stamp, the oneness, of a human being living in time and space but for a while. What my student clearly perceives is that the medium is indeed indistinguishable from both the message and the messenger. The mystery of our humanity is locked within the secret origin of our symbols. To use them, as a means of "indicting a good matter" of the heart, as the Psalmist puts it, is to exercise a privilege requiring careful attention to nuances of truth and a readiness to reveal a message of hope spoken from the lips of a divine messenger, the word literally made flesh.

Psalm 46

"Be still, and know that I am God." (Ps 46:10)

I just finished reading an article by William Deresiewicz in *American Scholar* magazine about the importance of solitude as a requirement for leadership. "The ability to be alone with your own thoughts," says the author, "is one of the most important necessities of leadership." Deresiewicz believes that leaders must be able to think independently, creatively, and flexibly—qualities that can only be nurtured in the silent spaces of one's own being.[1]

I couldn't agree more. However, I would extend the writer's observations to suggest that one cannot develop as a full-fledged human being without the requirement of solitude. Solitude forces us to focus on the self under construction not afforded by physical and psychological noise.

Yet the marketing culture in which we live is designed to snag our attention at every available opportunity, forcing more of us to adopt strategies of multi-tasking just to complete what we feel compelled to do. Simple empirical observation suggests that most people can't do one thing well, let alone four or five things at the same time. But Deresiewicz doesn't stop there. He cites research showing that multi-tasking impairs cognitive functioning and that the more a person multi-tasks, the less effective he or she is at multi-tasking. Here is the author's statement on the matter in full:

> Multitasking, in short, is not only not thinking, it impairs your ability to think. *Thinking means concentrating on one thing long enough to develop an idea about it.* Not learning other people's ideas, or memorizing a body of information, however much those may sometimes be useful. Developing your own ideas. In short, thinking for yourself. You simply cannot do that in bursts of 20

---

1. Dersiewicz, "Solitude and Leadership," 4.

seconds at a time, constantly interrupted by Facebook messages or Twitter tweets, or fiddling with your iPad, or watching something on YouTube.[2]

Being able to focus and to make independent judgments are anathema to a culture of corporate proprietorship. However, these qualities are necessary to the making of human minds and souls. The early Christian mystics understood the need for retreating to the desert where they could encounter themselves and God in solitude. It's worth considering: in the presence of so much noise, distraction, and advertising, who will be left to detect the "still, small voice" of God whispering in the silent chambers of our hearts?

---

2. Dersiewicz, "Solitude and Leadership," 5.

Psalm 47

"For God is the King of all the earth: sing ye praises with understanding."
(Ps 47:7)

I'd love to sing the praises of God with understanding. The only problem: I don't understand much of anything these days, least of all the changes occurring in me. How best to describe it? I don't feel like my old self, nor do I care to. My old self was content to be idealistic, to fulfill its obligations without complaint, and to ignore its own desires in order to please others.

Maybe my old self is used up. Maybe there's no more left of it. My old roles as husband, father, teacher, and writer no longer signify in precisely the same ways they once did. Time is the major reason, of course. I've changed over time. The people around me have changed too. The hopes, ambitions, and passions I once indulged no longer have the patina—the sheen—of satisfaction they held for me. "How unsatisfying is life in the final analysis!" I want to shout. That's when Jesus' despairing words come to mind: "Eli, Eli, la-ma sa bach thani?" or "My God, my God, why hast thou forsaken me?"[1] When I recall those words, I can only conclude that Jesus must have thought it was all for naught. Hadn't he done everything right? Then why had it turned out this way? Was he tempted, just as Nikos Kazanzakis suggests he was in *The Last Temptation of Christ*, to conclude that he'd taken the wrong path and should have chosen the lower road, one imparting the blessings of wine, women, and song?[2] Did Jesus feel his old self die at the instant he declared, "It is finished!"?[3]

Maybe being an authentic self means giving up all pretenses of having been an authentic being or having lived an authentic life. Maybe finding

---

1. Matt 27:46.
2. Kazanzakis, *Last Temptation*, 1–506.
3. John 19:30.

PSALM 47

out who you thought you were wasn't the whole story is the way to discover "dying to self" which no one can anticipate at the beginning of the journey. Life makes all our vows meaningless, it would seem. Is it any wonder I find myself grieving for the last parts of me—disappearing like features of an oasis in actuality and potential?

Psalm 48

"For this God is our God for ever and ever: he will be our guide even unto death." (Ps 48:14)

Shakespeare tells us that "all the world's a stage" and that we're "poor players strutting and fretting our hour upon the stage" until we're heard no more. The Bard is suggesting, of course, that life is a play—a tragedy at some times, a comedy at others—in which we play the parts written for us by the divine playwright. Within the context of the play, we exercise free will insofar as our limited vision enables us to view options available to us. Because we are "poor players," limited beings, we experience remorse and regrets—little deaths that are the inevitable result of being human.[1]

Often these little deaths come disguised as anything but death, as Donald Hall describes in his poem "My Son, My Executioner," in which the poet recognizes that his son's birth portends a death Hall has not anticipated:

> My son, my executioner,
> I take you in my arms,
> Quiet and small and just astir
> and whom my body warms.
> Sweet death, small son,
> our instrument of immortality,
> your cries and hunger document
> our bodily decay. (1–8)[2]

Here the poet is struck by the profound paradox of death in life and how the two are inseparable. Most parents anticipate with joy the stages of his or her child's life: taking the first baby steps, entering school,

---

1. Ribner and Kittredge, *Complete Works*, 371.
2. Hall, "My Son," 1–8.

matriculating at college. With each of these, however, there is the attendant awareness that these changes define both a beginning and an ending.

Yesterday was our youngest son's birthday: he was twenty-five. My wife and I were reminiscing about what excited, frightened, and naïve young parents we were even though we already had plenty of experience. Despite trying to cherish every minute of his life with us, it has all passed in a flash before our eyes. As we held our newborn baby a quarter of a century ago, we certainly didn't anticipate a time when we'd be sitting in an empty nest, trying to figure out who we are in the absence of being parents of children. Impermanence is the iron law of life.

Yet, within this scheme of things, I found a bit of permanence the other evening. Our youngest was having dinner with us. I asked him to say grace, expecting him to recite the standard Catholic prayer for such occasions, beginning with the line, "Bless, Lord, for these thy gifts which we are about to receive . . ." Maybe he was just distracted, but what came out was a prayer I'd improvised for him when he was barely old enough to talk:

> God bless us.
> Keep us safe.
> Hail, Mary.
> Love Jesus.
> Forgive sins.
> Lord Jesus Christ,
> Have mercy on us.
> Amen.

That it had stuck all these years in his subconscious gave me a moment of intense joy. It dawned on me that what I thought he'd undoubtedly forgotten was hibernating in my son's memory until the moment the divine made good on its promise of love's return.

Psalm 49

"But God will redeem my soul from the power of the grave: for he shall receive me." (Ps 49:15)

Last night I was talking to Erik, my middle son, about change. His daughter, my grandchild Kristen, is off to college in a couple of weeks, leaving him, a single parent, home alone. All of us experience incremental changes. It's just that when those changes culminate in graduation into a new phrase of life, we're struck with a sense of awe at how the ground of reality can suddenly shift under our feet.

Today is the birthday of a good friend of mine. She'll be fifty-eight. I lag just a few months behind her. She's contemplating early retirement in a year, so I've already begun to anticipate what life at work will be like without her. Doubtless some young faculty member will occupy her office across the hall from me. Such is the nature of life's inevitable changes.

As for me, I find my preferences changing a bit. I love children, but I don't want to share the swimming pool with them, preferring early morning laps to mid-day mayhem at the local YMCA. You also know you're getting older when no one expects you to do the things you were once expected to do—even if you're still perfectly capable of doing them. When your adult children volunteer to read the map for you on vacation and write out directions so you won't get lost, that's a sure sign of change. Nor does change at a certain age offer a chance of changing back. There isn't much likelihood that my eyesight will actually be better this time next year.

Just as change is the nature of living, it is also the nature of dying. The two are inseparably linked. Death, however, is a change like no other, one unimaginable in a realm of small, gradual changes. It is a change into infinite changeableness, or unchangeableness. Who knows?

Psalm 49

What I do know is that change is an ever-present constant in this sphere of existence—the one thing I can count on. At times that fact is comforting, at other times, unsettling. What keeps me from coming unhinged is the divine assurance that change is a necessary ingredient of leavening for anyone wishing to taste the bread of life.

Psalm 50

"And call upon me in the day of trouble: I will deliver thee, and thou shalt glorify me." (Ps 50:15)

Since I stay in trouble, I call upon the Lord on a regular basis. Put another way, I don't just stay in trouble; I *am* trouble, a perpetual source of it. Just a couple of weeks ago, I wrote to a priest friend of mine living in another city. "Pray for me," I said. "I need it, as usual." I'm sure he took me at my word. Knowing me as he does, he'd know I was serious.

Murder, lust, vanity. Even when I don't commit these sins in the flesh, I commit them in my mind—in abundance, because the mind can conceal them successfully. The mind can be a far more dangerous place than the world. Milton said it best: "The mind is its own place, and in it self / Can make a Heav'n of Hell, or a Hell of Heav'n."[1] Most often, mine does the latter, indulging fantasies of a grandiose nature, designed to make me the hero of my own narrative, giving me the status of a god among mere mortals. When I put it that way, I can't help but laugh. The truth is that not one of us is capable of extricating ourselves from the simplest dilemma involving ourselves. We're mired in so many layers of falsehood and self-deception that we justifiably become the butt of humor to those around us. That's the trouble with being in trouble. We don't often know it until it's too late, far later than those closest to us who have no trouble seeing the snares we set for ourselves. No wonder God tells his troublesome ones to call on him, saving us the trouble of discovering that we can't do without him.

---

1. Milton, *Paradise Lost*.

Psalm 51

"For I acknowledge my transgressions: and my sin is ever before me."
(Ps 51:3)

Yesterday, my wife Linda and I drove our youngest son, Gabriel, now twenty-five, from Boca Raton, Florida, where we're vacationing, to Daytona Beach, where he took an early flight home owing to obligations of work. The more than three-hour trek one-way gave us all a chance to visit and catch up in a way we hadn't had an opportunity to do in a long time. Our son currently works for the Boys and Girls Clubs of America; and because he supervises the activities of young children, he has plenty of humorous stories to relate. For instance, one little boy said to him the other day, "Mr. Gabe, I don't like life." Startled by signs of angst and despair in one so young, my son placed his hand on the boy's shoulder. "Why don't you like life?" Gabriel asked. The little boy replied, "I like Cocoa Puffs better." Small surprises of grace everywhere! Still, there is a dark side to the work my son is doing.

"I don't know how much longer I can stay in this job," he admitted on the road yesterday. We'd heard enough stories about crime, abuse, and neglect to know what he was talking about. "You don't have to stay," my wife said. "Nothing is permanent."

We know he's been struggling with questions of what to do with his life—whether to move to a new city, enroll in graduate school, or teach abroad. Momentous decisions in a young man's life.

For a time, there was silence in the car, then an optimistic inflection in his voice: "It'll all work out for the best," he said with an assurance that surprised me.

We deposited him at the airport in plenty of time to catch his plane home, then headed back to Boca to resume our vacation—a substantial day of driving to be sure. However, I didn't leave the airport without first calling upon a host of guardian angels and saints to provide protection, travel mercies, ensuring safe passage for both my son and myself. In my mind I was insisting that things go flawlessly.

They didn't. The drive back was plagued by road construction and holiday traffic. Though fatigued, we did arrive safely at our condominium. However, Gabriel called to tell us that after four hours, he was still stuck in the Daytona airport because of travel delays associated with coastal storms, shutting down the airport at Charlotte where he was to board a flight for Knoxville, his final destination. "Don't worry," he said. "They're re-opening the Charlotte airport at 6:30 and will have us on board here by seven."

My stress level soared, despite the fact my son is a patient and experienced traveler, having spent a semester in Europe while in college. "Why," I grumbled to myself, "do I bother praying to all these agents of grace if they're going to be so slow in providing it?" Obviously, it didn't take much in that moment to shake my faith.

My son arrived home safely at 10:30 p.m. He called as we'd requested. His voice was strong, sturdy—indicating no signs of fatigue. When I sympathized with him for experiencing a long day in airports, he let me know he was having none of it.

"It happens to everybody," he reminded me in the same tone of voice he's used earlier in the day when he'd said, "It'll all work out for the best."

With that, I humbly begged forgiveness of those divine presences I'd called on earlier in the day, the ones I'd complained about, but who'd found a way to keep us safe on the road until our final destination came mercifully into view.

Psalm 52

"Thy tongue deviseth mischiefs; like a sharp razor, working deceitfully."
(Ps 52:2)

While on vacation day before yesterday, I had an experience reminding me how it feels to be misunderstood. My wife asked me to check out some lawn chairs and a beach umbrella at the office of the complex where we're staying. The office opened at 9 a.m. I arrived a bit early to find a woman and a man talking, apparently having just met. The man's teenaged daughter was in tow, as well. They were all comfortably perched on benches outside the office, discussing the teen's prospects for college while waiting for the office management to open the door. I stood, arms folded, waiting, too. I should have guessed they were there for the same purpose as I, but to tell the truth I wasn't thinking about it. Besides, there are plenty of reasons a person might be sitting outside, waiting to gain entrance to the office: to check out, to file a maintenance request, to access the Internet connection.

When the door opened, the people on the benches were still in conversation and slow to rise. I greeted the manager, a pleasant woman, with whom I exchanged pleasantries before stepping inside. The others followed.

"What can I do for you this morning?" the office manager asked me.

"I'd like to check out some beach equipment," I said.

"She was here first," the man behind me blurted.

I turned to find him glaring at me.

"Oh, I'm sorry," I said. "I didn't know there was a line. Please, go ahead."

That's when I realized that the man wasn't offended on behalf of the woman he'd just met. In fact, his body language was such as to suggest he would have knocked her down just to get to the rickety equipment leaning against a sliding glass door. He wasn't through, however.

"She was here first," he repeated, casting me a sidelong glare.

I wanted to say, "I understand that, Neanderthal. What part of my apology didn't you get?" Instead, I tried to offer a second reassurance: "I certainly wasn't trying to usurp her position in line."

Maybe it was the word *usurp* that did it. He glared again. That's when I glared back, letting him know in that silent exchange that my manners extended only so far and that I knew there were people, like him, who refused to be placated no matter how much a person apologized or tried to explain.

Later, while sitting at the pool, I fumed over the episode, re-playing it in my mind. I tried to see it from his point of view but wasn't very successful. After all, he'd rebuffed my apology and *chosen* not to accept the sincerity of my intentions. What was I to do? That sense of frustration fueled my anger. I recalled that he was overweight and out of shape, not the best situation if you're going to go around making aggressive gestures at people. Couldn't the fool see that I was in good shape, though he certainly had no way of knowing that I've been a martial arts instructor for almost thirty years. And so it went for an hour or more: injured feelings, respondent rage, and abiding despair at not being able to reconcile the image I have of myself with all the messy contradictions I was experiencing. Surely, I said to myself, Jesus must have felt some of these same things, too.

That's when I laughed—maybe out loud. I don't recall. But in some instant of grace, I realized I would never rid myself of all my contradictions, not in this lifetime at least. To try without the aid of the spirit, relying on my own will instead, would result in failure time and again. Accepting my contradictions was a necessary step in accepting the contradictions of other people and of being able to forgive them when they behave the ways I do. In that instant, the prayer I needed to pray sprang to my lips: "Lord, give me the humility to accept my contradictions and not to fret when I can't do what you, in your infinite mercy, never expected me to do anyway."

Psalm 53

"There were they in great fear, where no fear was." (Ps 53:5)

We worship fear, calling it God. Governments stay in power by inspiring fear in people, even exaggerating fears by stressing all the terrible things that will happen if those in power are no longer able to call the shots. When governments and other institutions insist that fear is the state of things, they are resorting to coercion and violence of their own. They are threatening to withdraw their "protection." Few dare to ask "Protection from what?" That question would expose the power mongers' real motives.

It is interesting how we can justify violence, growing comfortable with its "inevitability." Each new comfort is seen in a unique context as if no other historical occurrence had ever been viewed with such a patina of singularity. This fallacy of perception multiplies the number of "exceptions" in which "responsible" societies may use a lesser evil to destroy a greater one. This is where people on the "left" and "right" find a point of agreement. As peace proponent Jan Love points out, "Whether that cause is revolution or stabilizing the balance between the superpowers or defending human rights or protecting the market occurs almost as a matter of the context and one's convictions about it. The argument for the means is the same."[1]

What few people want to acknowledge is the propensity of institutions to create dilemmas that force people to take sides while paradoxically agreeing that violence is the only option. Unless we are willing to examine our own "good" intentions and to expose the shadowy aspects of many of our most cherished institutions (government, church), then we will fail to see that much of the evil that shocks us is the result of structures put in place to do "good."

---

1. Love, "Practicing Consensus," 4.

What I'm beginning to realize is that we can never afford the luxury of feeling "good" about ourselves or the causes we represent. Eternal vigilance is the price we have to pay for waking up in the morning. We can never say we've done enough for peace in our homes, communities, or countries. Recognizing our human limitations and tendency to create problems where none exist, we must be willing to embrace the complexity of our faithfulness, understanding our need for redemption and forgiveness and the corresponding need to extend these things to others as a sign of our oneness. Put in other terms, we can't ignore the suffering we cause each other, whether deliberately or not. The results are the same. Fear and understanding are mutually exclusive. It follows then that the more we understand, the less we have to fear and the more powerful we become—powerful enough to bear up under Christ's cross and all its awful contradictions.

Psalm 54

"Hear my prayer, O God; give ear to the words of my mouth." (Ps 54:2)

As a writer, I'm sometimes asked to read to local groups. I'm rarely screened beforehand; but such was the case yesterday when two women, sponsors of a reading group, asked me to lunch at a member's only club here in town. Arriving a few minutes early, I sat waiting for them in the lobby, watching the passing parade of mostly lawyers, stone-faced and self-important, show up on cue for a meeting of the local Bar Association. Then came the mayor and his entourage. Despite His Honor's being more than fifty, his face was unnaturally boyish—whether from never having a serious thought or Botox, I couldn't tell. His followers, however, showed all the signs of acute anxiety and chronic insecurity. The staff at the club scraped and bowed as if in the presence of royalty.

It was beautifully ironic since the book of mine the club had on display was about the abuse of power by local politicians in the 1940s and 1950s. It didn't matter. The mayor and the lawyers would never read it. Even if by some miraculous stroke they did, they wouldn't recognize themselves in it. That's the price of making unreal choices: Reality slips away.

As for the women—self-proclaimed doctors' wives and soccer moms—with whom I had lunch, I'd like to say I enjoyed my conversation with them, but I don't remember having one. The aging belle on my left couldn't stop answering her cell phone. The one on my right chattered about subjects I can only assume she finds endlessly fascinating: golf, charity events, a new football stadium. At one point, I had hopes. The talk shifted to children. However, the bubble burst when the women began describing a soccer match in which it became clear to me that the children were simply small, worried adults like their parents. As the women continued, I couldn't help wondering how long it would be before their husbands left them for younger, longer-legged aspirants to the Junior League. Some things are entirely too predictable.

If I sound uncharitable, so be it. People don't have to live in furnished souls. They can choose something else. Nor do I absolutely have to take their nonsense seriously. Indeed, I would be only too happy to empathize with their *genuine* plights. But as some people not only opt to be walking stereotypes, but actually derive enhanced status from the packaged identities they inhabit, I feel no compulsion to nurture their fantasies. For these fantasies can only be maintained at someone else's expense. To believe otherwise is an illusion, and we have gone too far in that direction already. To embrace illusion is to reject truth. Perhaps no one in recent times understood this fact better than Thomas Merton who wrote,

> From the moment Christ went out into the desert to be tempted, the loneliness, the temptation, and the hunger of every man became the loneliness, temptation, and hunger of Christ. But in return, the fit of truth with which Christ dispelled the three kinds of illusion offered him in his temptation (security, reputation, power) can become also our own truth, if we can only accept it.[1]

What we must also accept is that some people don't want to give up illusion for truth. They are deliriously attached to all the things they believe make life worth living. Sad to say, theirs is already a world of the living dead. All the contents of their universe—including themselves—are inanimate and purposeless. People are pushed around like machine parts.

Yet, here he is—a thwart to the best-laid plans: Jesus bidding us to come to the desert beyond the web of obsessions required by those movers and shakers who count on the world to be their oyster. A pearl at any price? Indeed, with what sweet and idiotic self-deceit we forget that the cross is the only reality in our lives and that God's mercy can come like a thief in the night to steal our most cherished illusions.

---

1. Merton, *Thoughts*, 36.

Psalm 55

"And I said, Oh that I had wings like a dove! for then would I fly away and be at rest." (Ps 55:6)

Yesterday afternoon I gave a commencement speech as part of my college's graduation ceremonies. I spoke on the ability of poetry to be life-affirming in a world too often enamored of death. Poetry, I said, is that which begs to be expressed, which rises up from the deepest wellsprings of our being to offer a secret therapeutic love that can't be bought or sold. Another way to say it is that poetry is what we're ultimately concerned about, what won't leave us alone because it's too important to be denied. Who of us hasn't lain awake at night trying to discern the pattern of our lives in the ceiling's texture only to be flooded with reminders of all the little deaths, failed loves, and humbling contradictions that define our mysterious existence? I concluded by noting that some things can't be marshaled, organized, or counted. They can only happen.

Later, as graduates streamed across the stage, one young man smirked: "Nice speech, but if we did what you wanted us to do, nobody would have a job." He was right. Nobody would have a job or feel the compulsion to do work because of some external threat. Such work is punishment, drudgery, misery. It has nothing to do with the Great Work to which all of us have been called. The manifestations of this Work may be different, but the essence is the same for everyone. Thus, our real work is a holy quest.

Such a view takes work out of the here and now and places it in eternity. What is the genuine nature of our labors? No less than soul making. Only when we consent to accept that the world is machine-like and that we are parts to be pushed reluctantly into place, do we lose sight of work's great purpose: to give us insight into the divine workings of God. Work isn't a thing; it is the heart's attitude toward the uncreated universe that begs to be created. Least of all is work "a Darwinian sense of competitiveness and a Newtonian parts mentality," as Matthew Fox observes.[1]

Rather, our work calls us to be and to love and to give God a place within to do his work. This is what true poverty means: We empty ourselves so that God can continue to create our unborn being in his own image and for all time. Anything else is a conjurer's trick, an attempt to turn base metal into gold when God makes clear that our value as co-creators of a constantly created kingdom lies within.

---

1. Fox, *Sins of Spirit*, 306.

Psalm 56

"For thou hast delivered my soul from death." (Ps 56:13)

A friend of mine, a professor of religious studies and a Buddhist, remarked last week to me that Christianity had a serious theological flaw: "If you don't get it right the first time—and who does—then you're doomed for all time." Other religions, especially Hinduism with its successive incarnations, offer human beings countless lifetimes to get it right, he noted. "That's mercy?" I quipped. "If there's one thing I don't want to do, it's to do it again. What despairing tedium!"

Both of us laughed, going our separate ways and doubtless thinking our separate thoughts. As for me, I could see my friend's point though I tend to believe he gives Christians too much credit for understanding Christianity. What most adherents call Christianity is a form of *mass damnata*, a grim and dualistic Calvinism that damns some and saves others in one sweep. In fact, these people depend on such simple and deterministic "justice" to ensure their salvation. They demand that God be logical and consistent. No wonder they view him as a trickster when he surprises them, opening doors they've already closed, exposing their systems as shams.

They'll say they're only reading God's word, that Scripture is the source of their beliefs. What they're doing is reading themselves into Scripture. If the Bible teaches us anything, it's how prone we are to interpret the will of God in terms of our own projections. We know God's mind better than he does. What *does* the Bible show us if not how God thwarts our savage consistency in ways too mysterious to fathom? The cross is the chance for salvation we would never give ourselves.

No, my friend has succumbed to the temptation of seeing Christianity as a closed system marked by a changeless despair. He joins many Christians in believing this fallacy. Yet, God never gives us laws unless we ask for them, and even then he's reluctant, knowing how we'll use them to condemn others. What smug mischief we do in our heartless adherence to laws!

Still, if we're open to the possibility, then God is more than willing to destroy justice in favor of mercy. The last thing he wants us to believe is that he has locked all doors, given one answer, settled everything and departed, leaving us to our own merciless devices. With regard to that earlier theological dilemma and the "solution" offered by other, more "just" religions, I can only say how it seems to me that Christ has cancelled all our karmic debts stretching back to the beginning of time and extending into eternity ("I am the Alpha and the Omega."). If what I believe is true, it will constitute a scandal for some, good news for others.

Psalm 57

"My soul is among lions: and I lie even among them that are set on fire, even the sons of men, whose teeth are spears and arrows, and their tongue a sharp sword." (Ps 57:4)

All times are desperate in their own way, and our time is no exception. What characterizes our age? A madness that takes itself seriously, that fosters delusions and obsessions that require extraordinary expenditures of energy to maintain. Is there anything more exhausting than the self's efforts to promote itself above all other selves? Who are we trying to impress? The answer: anyone who can be taken in by us. The result is, in Thomas Merton's words, "an awful pattern of lusts, greeds, angers, and hatreds which mix us up together like a mass of dough and thrust us all together into the oven."[1] We can't even have a rational conversation anymore. Go to a party and notice the lupine expressions on people's faces. What can we learn from them? That human beings are to be devoured and disposed of when they no longer serve a useful purpose.

Never in my lifetime have we needed the scholar-warrior more than we do now. His or her words are needed to slice away falsehoods and to impart reason to a fanatical world. Such a warrior will not shun conflict in the service of truth. He or she will call a thing by its right name, no matter who's offended. Most important, the scholar-warrior won't succumb to flattery, honors, or the admiration of others since these things offer a temptation to forsake one's moral courage.

Some people would maintain that the scholar-warrior is woefully out of fashion. I would maintain there's no greater evidence of the need. Our first line of defense against the lies we tell ourselves is a language that won't

---

1. Merton, *Thoughts*, 37.

let itself be denied, that refuses equivocation. Connie Zweig describes how such language comes into being:

> My pen is *bokken*, sword of discrimination, ruthless as it follows certain lines of thought onto the page and ignores others into nonexistence. My pen gives life or death to words. My pen cuts through partial truths, slashes weak verbs and, sparring and paring, uncovers a rare, gemlike image. My pen knows the ancient practice of 'Neti, neti,' not this, not that.[2]

Writer Ishmael Reed puts it slightly differently. He says, "Writin' is fightin.'"[3] And no less than St. Augustine calls writing a "contest" in which the writer must wrestle to discover "visible forms of an invisible grace."[4]

Who would deny that gracelessness describes much of the language surrounding us today? The reason? It is language without truth and therefore without beauty. Yet, how can there be truth when there are no truth tellers and no one willing to listen even if there were? Scholars of the Middle Ages note that in past ages just such conditions inspired the rise of the scholar-warrior. Of these, the most famous was King Arthur. Who was Arthur? He was no single person; he assumed a different incarnation in every age. Several of him could walk the earth at once, often in disguise. His appointed task: to expose lies and to restore words as manifestations of the divine word. Like the one who came before him, Arthur did not fail to answer the call when forces conspired to ensure that the hour had grown late.

---

2. Zweig, "Becoming," 113.
3. Reed, *Writin' Is Fightin',* 1–225.
4. Augustine, *Confessions,* 217.

Psalm 58

"The righteous shall rejoice when he seeth the vengeance: he shall wash his feet in the blood of the wicked." (Ps 58.10)

Yesterday the Ku Klux Klan was protesting Gay Day at a nearby amusement park. A radio shock jock declared American teachers to be idiots, calling for our mass decapitation. A veteran police officer of thirty-five years was charged with raping a twelve-year-old neighbor girl.

To quell my anxiety and rage over these events, I went to a movie advocating the apocalyptic destruction of America for its sins against humanity. Recalling another news item in which a three-year-old Palestinian girl had been shot to death in Gaza while on a candy run, I decided that there was enough evil to go around for everybody and that finger pointing only compounded the problem. Maybe that's what Jesus meant when he warned us to "resist not evil." Maybe in doing so, we just add to the din of accusations and recriminations that keep the cycle going.

All I can say is that the Devil must be pleased with our assembly line responses and uniform self-justifications. They must provide him considerable amusement, especially at a time when everyone has an opinion and is a self-professed expert. Who really tries to understand anyone else? Who realizes that this is the first step in being understood?

I awoke last night, as I often do, rehearsing all the failed loves and humiliating contradictions that trouble me in the witch's hour of my sleep. Oddly, two quotations popped into my head. The first one was that "the quality of mercy is not strained."[1] The second one: "The best lack all conviction, while the worst / Are full of passionate intensity."[2] I wondered where the divide is between moralizing and being a moral coward. The

---

1. Ribner and Kittredge, *Complete Works*, 1491.
2. Yeats, "Second Coming," 7–8.

church calls us to be witnesses to both compassion and justice. I'm just not sure what sort of hypocrite I'm being when I believe I'm being compassionate or what kind of fool I am when squawking about justice. Omission or commission. Does it really matter if I can't stand my own company, let alone anyone else's?

Psalm 59

"But I will sing of thy power; yea, I will sing aloud of thy mercy in the morning." (Ps 59:16)

What is aging if not a narrowing of the path—a clarification of lost options and steadfast possibilities? Last night I dreamed I was in high school but woke this morning to discover I'm fifty something with a somewhat hazy history of events behind me. When I was young, I'd laugh at the bewilderment of older people who wondered where all the years had gone. It seems now that they can have the last laugh. One of the difficulties in aging is that you've heard and seen much of it before. No wonder some few drop out and become recluses. The din of the familiar is just too much to bear.

Once those seeking sanctuary fled to the desert. Now the desert has been appropriated as real estate. The journey has to be taken within, and there are few signposts to keep us on the path. Finding life amid so much death, Jesus tells us, is difficult. Ironically, it requires us to empty ourselves of all life's desires and enthusiasms that prove sterile in the end. Only the hearty or the insane are inclined to seek the Holy Grail on such terms. Anyone who believes that God never presents us with more than we can endure is deluded. The mental health facilities and the cemeteries are full of people who can bear witness to what I'm saying.

So how does one avoid the windy, sand-swept landscape that finds, in William Butler Yeats's description, "An aged man is but a paltry thing, / A tattered coat upon a stick"?[1] I, for one, don't want to be a spiritual scarecrow, detritus of a wasted journey, far from the comforts of home. Yet, I know too that only in such solitary places can one discover the awful presence of God. Even then, there are no guarantees as evidenced by Jesus

---

1. Yeats, "Sailing," 9–10.

who dies deserted and complaining, thinking the whole thing to have been a failure.

Psalm 60

"Thou hast shewed thy people hard things: thou hast made us to drink the wine of astonishment." (Ps 60:3)

The Psalms do not hesitate to show us the many moods of God. They also demonstrate that God is real, not something to be bent to our wills. In fact, the only time we are guaranteed of being on safe ground is when our wills accord with his.

Yet, too often the image we have of God is of a milksop. We emphasize the extent to which we can know God, forgetting what we can't know. In one breath the Psalmist praises God for his loving kindness; in the next breath he reveals God to be one who can "make the earth to tremble." It seems we've all too conveniently forgotten this "wild" side of God. Thank God for us that he can't be manipulated as easily as we'd like to believe. He is as hard and soft as water and as indestructible as light. To try to discover him is to discover ourselves in him—little more.

Even better than the Psalmist, at times, the Chinese philosopher Chuang Tzu captures this notion. Being in God was not accomplished by adherence to certain fixed rules and external standards. Being in God was forgetfulness of these things, as "when the shoe fits, the foot is forgotten." Christ, too, will often manifest contradictions unless we understand that this is the result of our way of seeing, not Christ's way of being. From the perspective of Chuang Tzu's Tao, or "Way," Christ exhibited no contradictions.[1] His many moods, like God's, were reconciled in the oneness of spirit. Only because of our atomistic thinking would it seem otherwise. We forget that by insisting on being reasonable, we are pushed to the brink of unreasonableness. By insisting that God conform to rules and ready-made conceptions, we create the extremes by which our rules and abstract

---

1. Chuang Tzu, *Way of Chuang Tzu*, 1–109.

formulations are shattered. These rules exist only for the spiritually immature. They are meant to be outgrown, shed as a serpent's skin. Only in this way can the new people of the Scriptures emerge. They are born of evil and good alike. (Have we forgotten that only someone susceptible to temptation can be tempted?) The new person lives without a thought for such categories.

Psalm 61

"Hear my cry, O God; attend unto my prayer." (Ps 61:1)

I have a small group of students—mostly, but not exclusively young men—who seem to experience separation anxiety at the end of each semester. They leave me phone numbers where they can be reached, soliciting promises that I'll read any future work they complete. I'm happy to read their projects, so the end result is that I maintain connections with these students, sometimes for years.

Because I am old enough to be a parent to most, I'm not imperious to the need many students have to be parented—something they have not received in adequate measure. It is a sad fact, but for all our emphasis on the cult of the child, we have sorely neglected a generation of young people. We've been too busy, indifferent, and self-obsessed to pay attention to them in ways that matter. What a sad and destructive legacy we have left them.

In one of my classes last semester, a young man named Russell couldn't find the ending to a screenplay he was writing. It came halfway through the term when his estranged father died from acute alcoholism. Another student, Patrick, displaying symptoms of ADHD, didn't know where he'd be staying this summer—maybe with his mother and her boyfriend, maybe with his millionaire father living in another state. I should make clear that I'm not judging the parents in these specific cases. I'm simply pointing out that our lives are intimately and tragically interconnected. The shortcomings of the fathers and mothers are heaped on the heads of the children.

Not long ago I was asking members of a class to recall a time when parents, grandparents, or other caretakers had read to them when they were small. Several of my students insisted that no one—not a single, solitary soul—had ever read to them. In my shock and naïveté, I said I didn't believe that. Surely, they just didn't remember. Only when I observed that my disbelief was being perceived as smugness did I grant them the validity of their experience. It was not my place to call attention to what they lacked through no fault of their own.

Nor am I in any position to ride the high horse when it comes to parenting. Although I read to my child, I'm sure I've failed him in other, countless ways. No, we are all a convocation of the guilty. Not one of us is innocent of the harm done to others. We collude by our very human nature, which is all too oblivious to its own motives. The only remedy for this situation is forgiveness, knowing that freedom results for all of us if just one of us does the unthinkable. The effects of such a thing could alter time itself, shrinking hell to an instant, expanding joy for all eternity.

Psalm 62

"How long will ye imagine mischief against a man?" (Ps 62:3)

If the veil were raised for an instant, would we not all see that we are literally brothers and sisters? Just yesterday I was driving in a poor section of town, careful to avert my eyes from people on the street, hypervigilant to the possibilities of danger around me. Truth to tell, I couldn't wait to get back to the "safe" part of town. What a sad indictment of me and all my contradictions and hypocrisy. Divisions of class, wealth, race, and nationality are so ingrained in us as to comprise emotional and psychological boundaries every bit as solid as rock walls. We reside in ghettos of poisoned thought and suspicion.

On my walk around the lake today, I couldn't help thinking about a word that has gained much currency in present times. It is the word *stereotype*. In writing about our confirmed desperation, Thoreau observes "a stereotyped but unconscious despair pervades all areas of our lives so that we can only respond in predictable, pre-packaged ways. We are enslaved to a global imperative insisting that the affluence of the few be purchased by the misery of the many."[1] Or as contemporary writer Morris Berman puts it: "What do we think it means when we buy a new sweater and the label reads 'Made in the Philippines' or a radio stamped 'Made in Korea'? What do we imagine the social and economic reality is behind these seemingly neutral words?"[2]

My answer? We don't imagine this reality unless forced. And usually such coercion comes in the form of economic upheavals or boycotts or politicians telling us we must fight to "preserve our way of life." What way of life is that? One in which images and slogans and corporate groupthink set

---

1. Thoreau, *Walden*, 1–4.
2. Berman, *Twilight*, 65.

out to destroy all vestiges of individuality or spirituality? The forces behind this conspiracy want us to forget there is any other way but theirs. They want us to believe there is no culture but the one they've created through systematic promotion. Again, Berman puts his finger on it: "Content doesn't really matter, because it is always the same: slogans work; hype is life. Virtual reality is not merely a cyber phenomenon, in short; rather, it defines the medium on which we swim, and from within this culture, there is no escape." The result, says Berman, is that "this phenomenon of the 'skin' of mass consumerism shows up everywhere, for we have become a nation unable to think except by means of slogans."[3]

If this is true, and we have embraced corporate categories to the detriment of reality, then the essence of spirituality is in danger of transforming into something hideously unrecognizable. Our only option, it seems, is to remind people of their birthright as human beings. To our children we must emphasize that a genuine spirituality is most often working against the grain and that being a spiritual warrior has nothing to do with ramifications of culture. Not one of our real spiritual heroes will resemble the actor asked to play him or her in the movie at the theater. In short, we can't afford the luxury of mistaking hype for reality if there is to be a reality.

The Chinese philosopher Chang Tzu offers us a way to tell the difference:

> What the world values is money, reputation, long life,
> achievement. What it counts as joy is health and comfort
> of body, good food, fine clothes, beautiful things to look
> at, pleasant music to listen to.
>
> What it condemns is lack of money, a low social rank,
> a reputation for being no good, and an early death.[4]

We might go so far as to call Chang Tzu a prophet in the way he anticipates and describes the lives of Jesus and his disciples. If we need more clarification, Jesus himself provides it in the Beatitudes where he challenges the grim corporate determinism of his day:

> *Blessed are the poor in spirit,*
> *for theirs is the kingdom of heaven.*
> *Blessed are they who mourn,*
> *for they shall be comforted.*

---

3. Berman, *Twilight*, 67.
4. Chuang Tzu, *Way of Chuang Tzu*, 12.

Psalm 62

Blessed are the meek,
for they shall inherit the earth.
Blessed are they who hunger and thirst for righteousness,
for they shall be satisfied.
Blessed are the merciful,
for they shall obtain mercy.
Blessed are the pure of heart,
for they shall see God.
Blessed are the peacemakers,
for they shall be called children of God.
Blessed are they who are persecuted for the sake of righteousness,
for theirs is the kingdom of heaven.[5]

---

5. Matt 5:3–11.

Psalm 63

"They shall fall by the sword." (Ps 63:10)

My son Gabriel, now eighteen, has been perfecting his skills and developing his own kata with the samurai sword I gave him a while back. It is remarkable what control and skill he exhibits. At times he stops and says, "This sword work isn't easy," acknowledging his awareness of all the metaphorical possibilities the sword represents. He senses that there are unplumbed depths to this activity that could only be discovered in a lifetime. In short, one's relationship to the sword is like one's relationship to a poem. If I treat the poem as an object, it will afford me few secrets. And while I may pass harsh judgment on the poem, the poem is also passing judgment on me for my obtuseness or lack of proper sensibility. Likewise, the sword holds up a mirror showing what sort of spiritual warrior I am. Now this protocol is what the sword requires: that it be treated with integrity and not used merely as an extension of my ego. In fact, to use the sword properly is not to use it at all. Better not even to pick it up if one isn't willing to put aside one's tiny self for the larger self we are destined to become. The sword as a form of active meditation gives us a glimpse of this self if we let it. That's why I enjoy watching my son wield the samurai. It is prayer in his hands.

Psalm 64

"Who whet their tongue like a sword, and bend their bows to shoot their arrows, even bitter words: That they may shoot in secret at the perfect: suddenly do they shoot at him, and fear not." (Ps 64:3–4)

The problem of evil is always with us, and I despair of ever understanding its sources. What I know is that there are people who insist on hating and being intolerant and, for some reason, feel no compunction about trying to bend others to their wills. Even now at my college, there is an intense young man in his thirties, a veteran of the military, who makes a point of subtly harassing a friend of mine, a middle-aged woman and fellow faculty member, who is also a sponsor of Pride, a student gay rights' group. The first time the young man in question made himself known to this woman, I intervened, confronting him directly. He is irrational, and an observance of civility means nothing to him. He feels under no obligation to respect anyone's authority but his own.

Such sociopaths make life unpleasant and potentially dangerous for the rest of us. In my exchange with the young man, it was clear to me that the only thing standing between his ferocity and my friend was the unspoken threat of force that I posed. I didn't want to be in the situation. I deplore having to stand in that place because of someone's Godzilla-sized ego and absence of conscience. But I didn't know what else to do.

I want to live peacefully, and I will exercise as much restraint as someone will let me. But I will not tolerate bullying of those unable to defend themselves against the viciousness of those who don't give a thought to hurting others. I will just have to deal with the spiritual discomfort of being the sort of person I don't like. God forgive me, but I've never known a bully to back down of his own accord. Going out of one's way to avoid such people only seems to bring them out of the woodwork.

I try to keep in mind that this young man isn't the first, nor will he be the last, to believe that special accommodations are required for his moods and demented thinking. I also recall the Psalmist's assertion: "So they shall make their own tongue to fall upon themselves." As for me, I need to wrestle with my own dark passions over this one. An enemy teaches us much about ourselves that we'd just as soon not know. What's increasingly obvious is the extent to which I can't afford the luxury of such ignorance.

Psalm 65

"O thou that hearest prayer, unto thee shall all flesh come." (Ps 65:2)

Yesterday my wife and I sponsored a living room dialogue for a group of international peace builders. Four in all, three men and one woman, they'd come to the US from India, Nepal, and Myanmar. After pleasantries, the conversation settled down to America's role in world affairs, especially our penchant for involving ourselves in wars in faraway places. The visitors wanted to know whether the American people were as bellicose as their leaders.

I said that I was sorry to have to admit it, but I suspected most Americans supported the current war for reasons only vaguely familiar to them. "But don't they know what effects these wars have on our countries?" asked a Harvard-educated doctor from Myanmar. "Most don't even know where your countries are located," I said. They looked stunned. "Keep in mind," I continued, "that one in ten Americans can't locate the United States on a map. Only 40 percent of graduating high school seniors know in what century the American Civil War took place. And only one in six Americans reads one book a year, with book defined as a mystery novel or Harlequin romance."

Clearly my guests were embarrassed for me.

"So, you see," I ventured. "Americans are not acquainted with the long-standing traditions of democracy and literacy that were once the benchmarks of our society. If anything, many Americans now have contempt for these traditions."

"Then why do they insist on thinking that they're patriotic?" the young woman from India asked.

"Unfortunately, Americans no longer think in anything but slogans—the by-product of our insatiable habit of believing our own marketing hype. Critical thinking is at a standstill."

"But what you Americans don't seem to understand is that we in other countries admire your democratic traditions and look to you for inspiration," said the man from Nepal. "That's why it's so hard to defend the action of your country to our neighbors when you engage in preemptive strikes and torture of prisoners. We expect such atrocities from petty dictators but not from the greatest democracy in the world."

They wanted me to assure them that only a minority of Americans supported such heinous actions and that the majority of our populace was peace-loving.

"I wish I could do that," I said. "I'm not sure I can."

With that grim admission of uncertainty, the talk turned to conditions in their own countries. In particular, the young man from India, who had spent time there in a Jesuit seminary and who now ministered to refugees from Sri Lanka, remarked on the severe problem of child prostitution in his part of the world.

"Poor families will sell a child for two or three dollars. The children will be forced to become prostitutes even before they reach puberty. The unfortunate result is that many HIV patients still believe the misconception that they can be cured by having sex with a virgin. AIDS then spreads back and forth from the adult to the child population."

"How does Western tourism contribute to the situation?" I asked, recalling how I'd recently heard a conservative radio commentator argue that American businessmen shouldn't be convicted by the legal system for having sex with children in other countries.

"It's a factor. Westerners on holiday have no qualms about partaking in these activities. They even justify them by saying they're contributing to the countries' economies. Of course, everyone knows that Bangkok is the worst city in the world for these transactions."

For a while we all sat in silence, trying to embrace the enormity of the situation. Unsuccessful, we at last began sharing our ironic perspectives of the human situation.

"In our part of the South," I said, "we have people who handle poisonous snakes as part of their religious observance."

"I bet they never tried to handle a cobra," said my friend from India. "Let them come to India. We have plenty of snakes they can handle!"

We laughed and ate and continued to talk until our time together was over. Knowing we would probably never meet again, we hugged each other, hoping we'd given something important and lasting to one another's understanding.

On the way out the door, Ashtok, the young Indian social worker, thanked me for my hospitality.

"If there's ever anything I can do for you . . ." offered this young man from one of the poorest places on Earth.

"There is one thing." He appeared surprised but happy to oblige.

"What's that?"

"Pray for us," I said, betraying an instant of anguish.

He smiled and nodded with what I could only guess to be a recognition of contradictions that trouble the sleep of children everywhere.

Psalm 66

"How terrible art thou in thy works! through the greatness of thy power shall thine enemies submit themselves unto thee." (Ps 66:3)

We wage war and call one another enemies, but surely the truth of our natures requires us to pause and look to the enemies within. Not knowing who they are or what hold they have over us only makes us vulnerable, isolated, and anxious. So I would like to take this opportunity to objectify those opponents who keep me shackled to my fears. If I recognize and befriend these entities, then perhaps we can co-exist peacefully, moving toward a oneness of spirit we have thus far been unable to achieve.

The first enemy I should probably try to befriend is one I'll term *hypersensitivity*. This enemy sets off all sorts of alarms in the face of perceived threats and slights, making it difficult for me to hear the truth about myself. People are therefore reluctant to tell me the truth for fear of my reaction. This enemy wears another face I call *shame*. How often was I shamed in my childhood by the very people who should have protected me from having to feel shameworthy? My response to this situation—an instinct for survival, in short—was to fragment myself, creating a piece of me that could weather the assaults. But that piece was wounded—hence its hypersensitivity to criticism or even the ameliorative effects of truth. It comes back to me now that I used to own this part of me as a friend—not as an enemy—but that I grew ashamed of him. I take him back now, realizing that he served me well in once helping ensure my survival but that he should now enjoy a much-needed rest. My enemy is my friend.

Another of my opponents takes the form of perfectionism—a standard by which I am secretly able to find others lacking. If I create the means by which people disappoint me, then I won't be disappointed when they do. I won't feel any obligation to extend them grace. Up 'til now, perfectionism has been the shield guarding my weaknesses. It was a way I could prove and protect myself from the earliest efforts of my mother to make me appear stupid or uncouth. Taunting me about my grammar, she ensured that I became a grammarian. Ignoring the basic needs of my body, she guaranteed that I became an athlete. "Doing all things well," as one friend described me, was insurance against criticism, or so I thought. Although perfectionism has served me well at times, it often drains my energy by forcing me to take on enormous tasks. For this reason, I would like to let go of the fear that drives me to perfection in all things and drives the people around me crazy, while acknowledging at the same time that being able to do a thing well is a gift. Therefore, I'll seek to lend this impulse a gentler perspective and more balance so God doesn't have to work so hard on my behalf.

The last of my opponents I'd like to confront is one I call the *Good Little Boy (or Girl)*. He is so good he won't defend himself. He defends everyone else, often to his own detriment. Part of the problem is that he has to feel good and not guilty about himself at all times. He is a vessel of other people's expectations, and they expect much of him. He's made sure of it. He's a sad little boy at heart because occasionally he would like to be at the head of the line instead of his accustomed place at the rear. He would like to have a piece of cake instead of the crumbs. But he feels that no one would like him if he were to demonstrate such *human* desires. When he was an even smaller child, someone once called him selfish, and he's been trying ever since to show that isn't true. No one notices him, and he shrinks each day for lack of proper nourishment. It goes without saying that he needs to be released from his self-imposed prison. Of all my "enemies," he is the one who needs my help most—who needs me to be his friend.

And so it is that these wounded parts of me have become my friends. To love something is to want it to live. I will give my friends back their lives and let them flourish in harmony with each other and with me until we all grow to be recognizable as one.

Psalm 67

"God be merciful unto us, and bless us; and cause his face to shine upon us." (Ps 67:1)

Sometimes I lie awake at night, surprised at the poignancy with which some events in my life resurface—things that, in some cases, I haven't thought about in years. That's when I have to remind myself that so and so happened twenty-five or thirty years ago. The stretch of time is real, but I can't make myself believe it. My life, at this point, seems to be of one weave, one fabric, and I'm grateful for it all, especially those times when the familiar seems mysteriously unfamiliar. I can honestly say that, for good or ill, I'm blessed to have a history that flows into the present and beyond. I have no desire to remake myself as so many of the self-help manuals encourage me to do.

It is enough to give praise for my small life that is part of a grand, unnamable, and unfolding plan in the mind of God who lets me be a part of his divine self. What I've come to realize is that none of us can be separated from that self. Division is simply an illusion. St. Elizabeth of the Trinity is quoted as saying, "My soul is a heaven where God lives."[1] If we take seriously the notion that God lives within us, then death is only a dream. There is no past or future. All time is now in the soul's eternal creation. Everyone who has ever lived or will live is joined to us in this interstice of time. Isn't that reason enough to give praise? All of me is one creation inseparable from ongoing creation and my soul's making.

---

1. Elizabeth of the Trinity, "My Soul," 1.

Psalm 68

"Thy God hath commanded thy strength: strengthen, O God, that which thou hast wrought for us." (Ps 68:28)

Yesterday a car repair turned out to be exorbitant. I had a moment where I actually thought of trading in the ten-year-old vehicle. Then I recalled how much more a car payment would be than a repair.

My spirits spiraled downward, and I felt ill the rest of the night. This morning I realize how little it takes to upend me, to bring me down from the pinnacle of whatever bliss I'm experiencing. There's a word for it: *mundane*, meaning "of the world." The world is always with us. We can't escape it. There are people whom the Holy Spirit has led into a dark forest. They know from whence their help comes because it can only come from one place.

This morning I am chastened when I think about all those people who don't own transportation, who don't have adequate nutrition or health care, and who are subjected to the most dispiriting kind of work if they have any employment opportunities at all.

For these reasons, I feel ashamed at my indulgent display of self-pity and my unwillingness to endure the slightest discomfort when I have brothers and sisters all over the planet who are living *in extremis*. My resistance to being one of them and to participating in their plight is appalling to me. What little strength is required of me to endure the small trials I face! What remarkable courage and nobility nameless millions demonstrate in the wake of life's assaults.

Psalm 69

"Save me, O God; for the waters are come in unto my soul." (Ps 69:1)

No one can escape the human condition. That is the lesson of the story of Job. If we are spared famine and poverty, then we will be besieged by diseases generated by excess from our so-called lifestyles. Likewise, our technological innovations ensnare us in a web of need for additional technologies to replace those that created the need in the first place. Built-in obsolescence. In the seeds of all our efforts are the fruits of our deaths. Living is, paradoxically, the means of our dying; dying is the reason we want to live.

The Psalmist recognizes that our lives are fraught with troubles, many of our own making. We possess insufficient knowledge but live in a universe that holds us responsible for what we don't know. Is it any wonder ancient humanity saw the gods as cruel and spiteful? It would not occur to early people to view them any other way.

But the singer of this psalm sees God in a different light—as God the caretaker and rescuer, archetypes springing from an impulse of love. Where did this notion of God's love come from? It certainly could not have been hatched in the minds of humans who were far more inclined to recognize their awful predicament and the gods who seemed to enjoy this state of affairs. Wish fulfillment—the projection and hope that a benevolent god does exist? That option hardly seems likely either. The ancient Hebrews did not live in a state of psychological fantasy. Their troubles and the troubling questions they asked were all too real. They experienced rage, frustration, numbness, fear—all things designed to quell faith or hope. Still, it appears that they believed in God not in spite of vicissitudes, but because of them: a startling paradox. How could a people so rational be so irrational if God's love wasn't every bit as real as the troubles they seemed never able to escape? Was one evidence of the other? If so, why?

PSALM 69

Still, the troubles persist—suffocatingly, making poverty not an emptiness or lack, but as a rising tide of concerns about to choke the hapless swimmer. The sense is one of being overwhelmed. Who has not experienced this sense? Who has not hoped for God who will "let not the waterflood overflow me, neither let the deep swallow me up, and let not the pit shut her mouth upon me"?

Psalm 70

"Make haste, O God, to deliver me." (Ps 70:1)

Recently an American businessman was decapitated by extremists in Saudi Arabia. He'd been held captive for days. Before his murder, his son went on television, pleading for his father's life. The young man wept, pointing out the obvious to his father's captives: "Please. I know some of you must be fathers, too." If so, they showed no evidence of the natural affections and concomitant sympathies that attend such a distinction.

While drinking coffee with a friend yesterday, I tried to express horror at a situation that will, unfortunately, be repeated. It is the sad logic of war that killing someone's father or son means someone else's father or son will be killed in return. People have almost come to accept this horror as a natural and inevitable state of things. After all, statism and hatred go hand in hand.

Lately, I've been disturbed by some of the theories being advanced about warfare and the human instinct to wage battle. One prominent psychologist guru argues that we've softened and refined the concept of war, creating such offensive and trivializing terminology as "the war on AIDS" or "the war on cancer." Apparently, war must sport a purer and most savage pedigree. Besides, war is energizing, say the experts, giving birth to some dynamic oppositions: love and hate, loyalty and betrayal, fear and courage. What could be more human than war with all its marvelous, soul-defining ambiguities? Even if some of us refuse to accept this line of thinking, we're stuck with the reality that war is here to stay. The horrors of war? Indeed, what about its pleasures? Is it really so hard to fathom that war, as the ultimate expression of the instinct for survival, is as indispensable as sex, perhaps even finding a blueprint for its continuation in the DNA? A war gene, in other words.

PSALM 70

Unfortunately, this rationalization does not accord with the image I saw on television of a young man grieving for his father. Even less does it conform to the spectacle of a sad father mourning for his son, unjustly sentenced to die on a cross in plain view of Roman soldiers. Neither of these scenes shares a penchant for the awful glories and man-making tests inspired by war.

Jesus said, "Blessed are the peace makers," thus throwing off war's yoke of determinism. His presence as God made peace possible in a way unrealized before. The extent to which we believe what he said is seen in our faith as peacemakers.

Yesterday, it occurred to me that what is needed is a worldwide network of People for Peace whose sole purpose is to protect all of us by ensuring that no one kills anyone else. This action would mean not succumbing to any government's propaganda, instead keeping our own minds while giving our hearts to others. If we were responsible for guarding everyone's children, including our own, then the joy of war would diminish, replaced by a seriousness of purpose and undertaking. Perhaps, in this way, no son would have to grieve for his father, or vice versa. And I would not be so perplexed as to wonder why anyone needs to consider such options on what the calendar fondly reminds me is Father's Day.

Psalm 71

"Now also when I am old and grayheaded, O God, forsake me not; until I have shewed thy strength unto this generation, and thy power to every one that is to come." (Ps 71:18)

Anthropologist David Gilmore argues that the glorification of material consumption lies in the universal association of manhood with material possessions. For some reason we've come to believe that a "real" man is someone who takes what he wants and is indifferent to the needs of others. What a far cry from the real Jesus who sweated blood and resisted temptation so that others might live. In the desert this Jesus is offered what "real" men in our society are supposed to be seeking with a frenzy bordering on mania: power, fame, and security. What this incident illuminates is how Jesus knew the devils in his day and our own. He offers a striking counterpoint to the idea that "real" men look out for number one, doing whatever it takes to acquire, in Gilmore's assessment, "ownership of valuable goods—land, cattle, or cash—and [in terms of] power over others, especially women and children."[1]

Jesus rejects this illusory notion of manhood. Instead, he *reminds* us that real men crucify those ambitions indulged for the sake of oneself. Real men give more than they take; they serve others. Real men are generous to a fault. They protect the weak and show respect to those whom other worldly men would never think of valuing. They willingly become the last so others, less fortunate or talented or blessed, can be first—if only for a single time. Why? Because everyone is deserving of God's love.

Real men know that God himself fulfills this lesser known and appreciated image of manhood. For God's strength resides in his willingness to share our weakness. His compassion pours forth from a heart willing to

---

1. Gilmore, *Mindfulness*, 10.

break like ours. His power stems from a desire to support the powerless. How we ever perverted this ideal or came to see it any other way ought to strike a chord of fear in those whose egos lead them to believe they are "real men."

Psalm 72

"He shall spare the poor and the needy, and shall save the souls of the needy." (Ps 72:13)

The anecdote is almost legendary. The brilliant Southern writer Flannery O'Connor found her mother reporting a neighbor's advice: "Tell that girl I wish she'd stop writing about poor people." To which O'Connor allegedly responded: "Tell him I didn't know there was any other kind."[1]

It was characteristic of O'Connor to go to the heart of the matter, not to let us cherish illusions in the face of more pressing spiritual realities. Consider: we all stand naked and poor before God. We are nothing without him.

Unfortunately, ours is a culture of perverse individualism that is contemptuous of interdependence and cooperation. Fostering the myth of the self-made individual, we forget that there is not one thing of our own making. Even our lives are a gift. That fact alone makes all our strivings unnecessary, just as Jesus reminds us: "Which of you by taking thought can add one cubit unto his stature?"[2]

Poverty of the sort I'm speaking of here requires the recognition of an emptiness that only God can fill. It's the reason Jesus also says, "Blessed are the poor,"[3] a testament to our humble origins and divine splendor. The degree to which we acknowledge our nothingness is proportionate to God's desire to bestow his blessings on us. Indeed, who of us can improve on the beauty of a child's smile, a hummingbird's mercurial flight, or the elegant shape of hands belonging to someone we love? How can any of these be described as constituting poverty?

1. O'Connor, *Letters*, 37.
2. Matt 6:27.
3. Matt 5:3.

Psalm 72

O'Connor grasped our essential condition. She knew that the psalms-up gesture of praise was identical to the one for receiving abundant blessings: both require empty hands. Not coincidentally, Flannery loved the spectacular plumage of peacocks. As a girl growing up in Georgia, she raised the birds, regarding them as creations of the divine imagination. Imagine being a midwife to such a creature! Maybe that was the secret the author grasped all along: to create is to be created. Put another way? To be in need of God is the only need we have.

Psalm 73

"Behold, these are the ungodly, who prosper in the world; they increase in riches." (Ps 73:12)

Anyone who believes that the "problem of poverty" is different from the "problem of wealth" is deluded. Our choices are interrelated; our whims and obsessions have consequences for people we don't even know. For these reasons, in her essay "Zen and Money," Ming Zhen Shakya has the following to say:

> Before buying anything we need to ask, 'Is this something I need or just something I want?' We should give desire a test time. 'When did I decide I wanted to make the purchase? Was it something I planned to buy and then went looking for, or did I decide I needed the item right after I saw it or its advertisement?' Impulsively made purchases are seldom appreciated beyond their time of novelty. So, especially with 'big ticket' items, we need to take time to get beyond the impulse, to free ourselves from being pressured into acting quickly.[1]

As I write this, I'm sitting in a beautiful, rented home in New Smyrna Beach, Florida, while on vacation with my family. Most of the people living in this resort town are affluent, retired, and sequestered. However, I came to know one of my neighbors yesterday in an unexpected way. On first arriving, we'd no sooner pulled into the driveway and exited the car when a voice called, "Help me. Help me." Its plaintive cry was repeated several times. Walking toward its source, I was hesitant to trespass the manicured lawn and almost turned around, especially when I couldn't see anyone. The voice came again: "Don't walk away. Help me."

---

1. Shakya, "Zen and Money."

Psalm 73

I trudged up the driveway, spotting a man partially concealed behind a palmetto bush. A double amputee, he had somehow managed to get the rear wheel of his wheelchair mired in some sand. Elderly, ill, and incapacitated, the man named Alan didn't know how long he'd been sitting in the sun, calling out for someone, anyone, to help him.

My wife jokes that I have a knack for showing up the instant people find trouble. As I remind her: "A magician is never not where he's supposed to be." The truth is probably that I'm hypervigilant owning to a neurotic temperament and an anxious childhood. Nevertheless, I'm confident God can use these deficits to his advantage.

Despite the brevity of our encounter, I came to know Alan and some essential facts. A widower who lost his wife to cancer a few years ago, Alan suffers from diabetes, having lost his legs to the insidious disease. Formerly a successful businessman from New Jersey, Alan lives with a fifteen-year-old poodle, Booky. A home health care specialist visits Alan daily.

In talking with him, I concluded that Alan has enough money to have all his needs met but the most important ones. He is one of the poorest of the poor. What does that mean, exactly? It means wealth, paradoxically, precludes our living in real community. It means there comes a time when consumption no longer fills a void in one's life. It means that, no matter how hard we try, we cannot escape suffering. That, alone, is the reason we need one another.

What poor, sad creatures we are! Our needs are legion; our egos are gargantuan. But in the final analysis, we, like Alan, may be forced to call on strangers to lift us out of the mire. I suspect that's what it takes to show us we're all one. Doubtless, it's a valuable lesson. If only it could be purchased in something other than the currency of suffering.

Psalm 74

"We see not our signs: there is no more any prophet: neither is there among us any that knoweth how long." (Ps 74:9)

Embedded in the consciousness of every human being is a triptych of questions: "Where do we come from? What are we? Where are we going?" It's our life's quest to seek the answers to these questions, for they not only define us but also our relationship with God—the extent to which he lives in us and we in him. Of course, no one expects to answer these questions in the same way one solves problems on an exam. That would be an absurd misuse of one's mind and an incomplete understanding of the sort of contemplation that ought to be the *summum bonum* of a genuine education.

Aristotle says we are born wanting to know. It's an innate impulse defining us as human beings. Nor can this impulse be separated from the questions God gives us defining his essential nature. He is the ground of being that can only be known to the degree we seek to discover our being in him. The flashpoint of this union of beings is Christ, or rather, universal Christ unconsciousness, the source of all love that is known.

That's why every human intention, every gesture and action, should be seen in light of divine contemplation. From this view, such activities as working a puzzle, tying one's shoes, or simply staring at dappled shadows on the ground are examples of being in the moment with God. These are also ways of asking questions for which we simultaneously discover the answers ("Knock and it shall be open to you. Seek and ye shall find.").

In his book *Christian Meditation*, James Finley puts it this way:

> The meditative awareness fostered and sustained in meditation will flash forth with ever greater frequency in all sorts of unexpected ways as you go through your day. You might, for example,

be standing at the sink doing dishes. As you look up, your heart is quickened in the recognition of God in the gentle breeze that barely stirs a leaf on a branch of a tree just outside your kitchen window. You interiorly smile back at God, grateful that you are no longer surprised by these little surprises.[1]

To be present in what we are doing at the moment is to be in communion with God—a blessed oneness reminding us that we can never be separated from him, no matter how much fear and confusion we experience. Like walking a labyrinth, the way in is the way out, enabling us to conclude whatever story we've begun in a way that makes all our questions suddenly make sense.

---

1. Finley, *Christian Meditation*, 33.

Psalm 75

"Unto thee, O God, do we give thanks, unto thee do we give thanks."
(Ps 75:1)

The ancient Hebrews are always seeking God, forgetting that God is both close and infinitely distant or that he is simultaneously concealed and revealed in the texts he gives us. God is his word, but his word demonstrates how much more than his word is God. Signs, dreams, and intuitions are indirect apprehensions of a God whose presence never assumes greater value than when he is absent.

For me, God seems remarkably absent in my dreams, ones which, under most circumstances, might be classified as nightmares. Last night, for instance, I dreamed I returned to my childhood home only to find it overrun by strangers. I tried to tell a neighbor what was happening, but the words he spoke were incomprehensible. I made certain not to wake my mother, fearing her furious response and dark moods. A voice kept reminding me I had nowhere else to live.

On waking, I found it hard to believe that I wasn't still stuck in that awful interstice in time when I seemed a stranger to myself and to other people. For many, there is no more confusing, chaotic, and alienating period than childhood. It's as if some of us sense we were born in the wrong cave.

Unfortunately, terrors of alienation don't always subside with childhood. Neither does the awful suspicion that God is nowhere to be found. The peculiar paradox was that he was never farther away than when I needed him. I soon found it unconscionable that he would abandon a child. I'm still not reconciled to the idea. It remains an issue between us, lingering evidence of a wound that refuses to heal.

Psalm 75

All I can say is the wound has made me a more compassionate person than I otherwise would have been. It also encourages a discourse that begins again and again because the distance between us remains. I find I must repeatedly begin speaking again to restate what I have said. The result is an inevitable, yet rich and blessed, redundancy.

All of this underscores an idea found in the work of Jacques Ellul:

> Dialogue involves a certain distance. We must be separated as well as different. I do not speak to a person identical to me. I must have something to say which the other lacks, but he must be different from me.[1]

Thus, to be distinct selves requires a distance and a difference, a mystery never fully understood. Only at the site of woundedness can God and I find a similarity that reconciles the gulf between us. Only the abandoned son of God narrows the distance between divine love and human suffering. He shares in my suffering, and I share in his. Together we watch the distant sun fading, leaving marooned mankind behind.

---

1. Ellul, *Humiliation*, 17.

Psalm 76

"Surely the wrath of man shall praise thee: the remainder of wrath shalt thou restrain." (Ps 76:10)

People love a hateful God. It is an expression of our inmost desire to reject a gift of freedom and to control others. Nowhere is this more apparent than in my students' response to Jonathan Edwards's famous sermon, "Sinners in the Hands of an Angry God," in which the Puritan divine writes that

> The god that holds you over the pit of hell, much as one holds a spider or some loathsome insect over the fire, abhors you and is dreadfully provoked: His wrath towards you burns like fire; He looks upon you as worthy of nothing else but to be cast into the fire; He is of purer eyes than to have you in His sight; you are ten thousand times more abominable in His eyes than the most hateful venomous serpent is in ours.[1]

When I suggest that Edwards has created a bully God, one born out of savage masochism and a projection of our desire to worship the worst aspects of ourselves, my students chafe, becoming angry at me for suggesting such a thing. They refuse to see it is our *own* wrath not God's that creates a living hell for us. God is pure love, indivisibly so, and is incapable of judging us, of separating us from him. Yet we cling to the notion of a God who rejects us the way we reject him. It's a perverse joy we experience in holding onto guilt and shame and the demi-god demanding these things of us. In fact, in our scheme of things, there exists no difference between God and Satan. They are the same person because they require essentially the same thing: bondage and servitude to impossible ideals. When we and others fail

---

1. Edwards, "Sinners," 390.

Psalm 76

to live up to these, the hell we've created awaits us. We wouldn't have it any other way.

Never mind that hell is a door locked from inside or that some people would be comfortable in hell itself. Why? Because we cannot separate God from our own dark nature. We require him to be just as vengeful, spiteful, and hateful as we. If God is this way, how can we expect any more of ourselves? Just like the Israelites in this psalm, we feel justified in calling down God's "wrath" and "judgment" on our enemies. We even chafe when Christ urges us to pray for our enemies, forgetting that we're praying for ourselves.

Psalm 77

"Hath God forgotten to be gracious? hath he in anger shut up his tender mercies? Selah." (Ps 77:9)

We don't really believe in forgiveness, or we wouldn't be so unforgiving. It's a simple proposition demonstrated by the fact that we find so many other responses preferable to forgiveness. Take *justice* for instance. Has any other word been so elevated or cherished? In the U.S., especially, people speak of *justice* in reverential tones, promoting it above all other virtues. Forgiveness is weak, suspect, by comparison. Forgiveness seems to admit all equivocation or pliancy of will.

We forget that the root of justice is *judge*. But even that is fine with us because being in a position to judge puts us in a superior relationship to what or whom we're judging. And, above all, we love feeling superior to the criminal, the poor, the less successful, the awkward, and the less self-confident among us. It is true: Our judgments have the power to diminish other people by forcing them to see themselves as we do.

Forgiveness requires just the opposite. It requires us to see ourselves as those we judge would see us. It means acknowledging our vulnerability and uncertainty. In order to forgive and to be forgiven, which are the same, we must give up the certain conviction that all our judgments are right. We must acknowledge the incompleteness of our understanding. In doing so, justice shrinks, assuming its proper place beside the infinitely larger prospect, the life-transforming virtue, of forgiveness. Who would not shout for joy on discovering that all his debts were forgiven, the account was closed, and that he owed nothing? What freedom from worry and anxiety each of us could experience if we no longer forced people and ourselves to adhere to impossible standards? The extent to which we're able to let go of our judgments is proportionate to our ability to perceive the "tender mercies" mentioned by the Psalmist. But as long as we judge people as enemies, we'll experience God as an enemy too, wondering why he has cast us off when the reality is that we prefer his judgment over his mercy, believing we get exactly what we deserve.

Psalm 78

"Then the LORD awaked as one out of sleep, and like a mighty man that shouteth by reason of wine." (Ps 78:65)

Too often, the God of the Old Testament is depicted as a passionate clown, a buffoon on high, who thunders "like a mighty man that shouteth by reason of wine." Yahweh smites so many people, friends and enemies alike, it's impossible to provide an accurate body count. Yet the Psalmist keeps telling us that God is good and merciful as long as we keep our covenant with him. In other words, there are limits to God's mercy.

A better way of acknowledging the truth of this situation is to say that there are limits to the human imagination. How else to explain why so few people in his time were able to recognize Christ's divinity even when he performed miracles like those attributed to the patriarchal deity of the Old Testament? Easier for us to believe in a god who's ready to clobber us at the first signs of resistance.

Someone asked me not long ago how I could be certain Jesus was God. Simple, I said. He never did anything ungodlike. He never judges; He never is selfish or self-absorbed; He doesn't require living sacrifices, offering himself as one instead. He isn't bureaucratic, hard-hearted, or totalitarian. About the only time he gets angry and stern is when he witnesses "the least of these" being shoved to their accustomed place at the end of the line. Even then, he asks the arrogant and powerful: "Do you know what you're doing? Do you know whom you're offending?"

It is not he who judges them but they who judge themselves—cutting themselves off from God—the bountiful giver of all that is good. We own nothing that God hasn't given. Nor can we earn or be deserving of a gift. A gift simply *is*. But who of us really believes there's a gift freely given since our murky and conflicted motivations rarely let us give freely, offering

Psalm 78

no thought of recompense? If you have trouble discerning this occurrence to be the case, then recall the last time in frustration you expressed some variation of the sentiment: "After all I've done for him (or her)!" To my way of thinking, only God has a right to say that. But then, God wouldn't think of saying such a thing. Giving freely, he'd have no need.

Psalm 79

"O remember not against us former iniquities: let thy tender mercies speedily prevent us: for we are brought very low." (Ps 79:8)

As philosopher Andre Comte-Sponville writes, "Forgiveness is an overabundance of freedom."[1] Ironically, that's why the Psalmist finds himself and his people in captivity. Their hearts are full of anger, hatred, and resentment. If truthful, most of us would have to acknowledge that forgiving others is next to impossible. We're shackled to our ball-and-chain history of grudges, insults, and inquiries. Often, these seethe just below the surface of our awareness. Still, most of what we have to forgive is forgivable if we're willing to do one thing: give up certitude for truth.

Who of us isn't convinced he or she is right most of the time? As such, we're quick to see others as wrong, evil, or wicked. The thought that someone else is at a different place on the spiritual path doesn't occur to us, or worse, is anathema to us. We fail to see that this response is the source of spiritual pride, a hubris that results in hatred of others. We forget that evil is a matter of will, not ignorance.

Mercy recognizes that no one chooses his or her body or history. For this reason, everyone requires sympathy. Not one of us escapes these limitations so that even the death of an enemy is an occasion for sadness and an opportunity for sober self-awareness. Imagine if being admitted to heaven required us to argue the case for admitting our enemy, as well. I suspect most of us would find some of the good we'd so studiously avoided. We'd certainly be more forgiving of errors resulting from ignorance, immaturity, and lack of imagination.

---

1. Comte-Sponville, *Small Treatise*, 122.

PSALM 79

That would be a start in helping us forget all but what really matters: We are one humanity beloved of God, in need of his "tender mercies" for all those times when we "are brought very low."

Psalm 80

"Turn us again, O God, and cause thy face to shine; and we shall be saved." (Ps 80:3)

Truth is not obedient; this is why it is free. Dogma is not truth, though truth can comprise some essentials of dogma. Owning no obligation to anything but itself, truth demands nothing other than that we pursue it. Nor does truth betray its seekers.

I was reminded of all this the other day when a student of mine, a young man named Jon, came to interview me for the college newspaper about my involvement with SNAP—the Survivors Network of those Abused by Priests. As a child, I was never abused by clergy, but I am faculty advisor for the campus Catholic organization at my college, and I think my church cannot continue to exist, nor does it deserve to, in the absence of serious soul-searching and the willingness to confront unpleasant truths about itself.

But the church is, foremost, a bureaucracy. It is a top-down organization characterized by a power structure with no vested interests in probing its weaknesses. Under no circumstance does power enjoy exploring its own shadow, its backside. It may convince itself it is willing to do these things, but that is the height of delusion and a manifestation of psychological blindness that can only be remedied by admitting light from without. Jesus never attached himself to power structures, pointing out how blind they are to their own motives. In fact, he championed the powerless, proclaiming them blessed, precisely because they were freed from any need to manufacture rationalizations or to conceal truth so as to appear being right. What a burden it is to have to be right all the time!

Moreover, Jesus drew the powerless to him, calling them his children, and cautioning the existing power structures to treat "the least of these" gently, or there would be hell to pay. Search the gospels carefully, and you will find that about the only people Jesus can't abide are bureaucrats and the hard-hearted. These are the ones who too often convince themselves of their own rightness. Jesus counters such "righteousness" by warning that God is the light that pierces darkness. Try to conceal a secret? In his profound mercy, God will open the door to the closet only to expose whatever monster is squatting there.

And yet, the church would make a fool of God by insisting we "forgive" pedophile priests whom we now know the church has harbored, rescued through exorbitant legal funds, and reassigned to parishes where people were unaware of former allegations and assaults. While a local priest tells students that "lust" between a husband and wife is sinful, I have yet to hear a homily in my diocese in which anyone admits the church has a serious problem with clergy abusing children.

Indeed, those of us who've expressed concern are told to forgive the former bishop of our diocese, a self-confessed pedophile still with the church until his death in 2012. Who tells us this? The new bishop, of course. He and other administrators even insist on keeping the former bishop's likeness in conspicuous places: the local Catholic high school and the diocesan office. The reasons for leaving the man on display are too embarrassingly feeble to repeat. He was later removed.

All of this creates in me a sense of dread because I do not believe a house divided against itself can long stand. I honestly can't imagine what will happen if church officials do not become as little children, willing to seek the truth at the expense of their own certitude. I suspect we'll continue to hear screeds on the necessity of forgiveness. And under the proper circumstances, I would be happy to hear them. But I recognize the dangers of sentimentality and "cheap" forgiveness of the sort the church's power brokers are asking me to display. To my way of thinking, that is akin to crucifying Christ's little ones twice. I refuse.

Rather, I will pray the church comes to its senses—eschewing arrogance and the unctuous face of public relations until a time when the church is sincere in asking forgiveness of its victims. Imagine the freedom! The church's leadership can let go of fear and defensiveness, embrace a sometimes difficult but genuine process of forgiveness, and accept the mercy of a God who doesn't care that we are right—only that we are true.

Psalm 81

"So I gave them up unto their own hearts' lust: and they walked in their own counsels." (Ps 81:12)

A poem by an unknown Irish poet contains the following stanza:

If generous men and women die out.
A poet loses his desire
To celebrate the noble hearts,
To praise all that they are. (Anonymous)

Poets and prophets stand alone, uttering a language many "understand not." The Psalmist certainly recognizes the correlation between a people's humanity and their ability to hear the voice that animates all entities with love. Not to hearken to this voice results in people "walking in their own counsels." They forsake the Tao, the Way, and the poetry of Being. This poetry is simply the distillation of the word for which no other words will suffice. It should not be confused with the noise we make all by ourselves. Perhaps no generation in history has been so in love with its own voice. It is my observation that you can now have a conversation with someone and never be forced to respond. We used to have a word for this: *megalomania*.

Is it any wonder that poetry is a tongue-tied orphan? No one will be quiet long enough to let her sign. Another way to put it is that great poetry requires great audiences. What has become of us? Are human beings in shorter supply than before? I have a theory: I believe people can now only tolerate language that equivocates—that exonerates us from things that make us feel guilty. It is a language that sells us on the worst aspects of ourselves. Anything else makes us furious.

That is why we crucify poets and prophets with our indifference. Before his death the poet James Dickey told his last college class: "The world does not esteem us much, but we are masters of a superior secret."[1] Well, that may be. But it is also true that we can refuse to hear even the secret of our own salvation. As Jesus repeats the words spoken by the prophet: "I will open my mouth in parables. I will utter things which have been kept secret from the foundation of the world."[2] Yet, when he took his living message to those most in need of it, being those least likely to hear it: "But he seemed as one that mocked..."[3]

---

1. Powell, "James Dickey."
2. Matt 13:35.
3. Gen 19:14.

Psalm 82

"God standeth in the congregation of the mighty; he judgeth among the gods." (Ps 82:1)

There is no more dangerous doctrine under heaven than election—the notion that God saves some while damning others. As one elderly friend told me recently, "There is a burning fire for those who don't accept Christ. Make no mistake about it!" She went on to estimate all the people she'd tried to convert who'd nonetheless been cast into a lake of fire, wishing for all eternity they'd listened to her. I wonder how many people would have to go to hell before she'd feel safe.

It is a grim scene, worthy of the worst excesses of the human imagination. Yet here it is in the first verse of the psalm: "God standeth in the congregation of the mighty; he judgeth among the gods." All creation quakes before the awful and terrible presence of God as he seeks the ultimate revenge. Yes, hell is born out of the heart's dark desire for retribution: getting even with those we refuse to forgive. Has anything in human history caused more mischief than this notion of *justice*? Separating the sheep from the goats—the end to an already cruel and sorrowful story in the annals of tortured human divinity.

How do we go about translating the woeful imagery of Judgment Day into a pure judgment of utility? Primo Levi tells us how it's done in his book, *Survival in Auschwitz*. First, believe you know God's will for both individuals and nations. That having been decided, you are now free to judge "a man whose life or death can be lightly decided with no sense of human affinity." Levi describes this contemporary day of doom:

> A dozen SS men stood around, legs akimbo, with an indifferent air. At a certain moment they moved among us, and in a subdued tone of voice, with faces of stone, began to interrogate us rapidly,

Psalm 82

one by one, in bad Italian. They did not interrogate everybody, only a few: 'How old? Healthy or ill?' And on the basis of the reply they pointed in two different directions. We had expected something more apocalyptic: they seemed simple police agents.[1]

As Mephistopheles admits in Marlowe's *Faustus*: "Why, this is hell, nor am I out of it."[2] Hell is the judgment we reserve for others, forgetting that we are all "children of the most high." Oddly, the Psalmist forgets his own counsel in all too typically human fashion, accusing God of judging "unjustly" and of accepting "the persons of the wicked." To this request that God do something immediately to remedy this situation, our Lord responds with merciful silence.

---

1. Levi, *Survival in Auschwitz*, 19.
2. Marlow, *Faustus*, Act 1. SC.3, 1.74.

Psalm 83

"They have taken crafty counsel against thy people, and consulted against thy hidden ones." (Ps 83:3)

It is almost impossible to hide—to be one of the "hidden ones" mentioned by the Psalmist here. Even the desert has been co-opted, used for various forms of advertisement and harassment. Just try to escape our commercial paradise and all its enticements. See how quickly you become an outcast in the society of consumers. You must stay "connected," we are told, via cell phone and internet, or you have no value. You cease to exist.

Where is the desert, then—that barren yet beautiful place chosen by God as the focus of revelation, an arena of soul making? It has been threatened by encroachment and an insatiable hunger for power over others in the world as it is now. Why have need of a desert when you can experience an "infinitely more ample, flexible, variegated, attractive oasis" where travel is "safer, less risky, and off-putting?" A place, as Zygmunt Bauman describes it, where "distance is no obstacle to getting in touch—but getting in touch is no obstacle to staying apart."[1] Connection, paradoxically, results in lack of connection.

The desert provides no such safety. It requires us to give up our impulsive desires to be connected by the shallowest means possible. It invites us to be united eternally to the inexpressible name of truth that brings us into being. It forces us to remove our masks and to take a closer look at our unfulfilled yearnings, ragged nerves, blank indifference, disappointed love, hurts, resentments, loneliness, fears, hypocrisy, egotism, and repetition compulsions. In short, all those things that refuse to disappear with the stroke of a *delete* key.

---

1. Bauman, *Liquid Love*, 100.

Psalm 83

Where is the desert? I know where it's not. Maybe that's a start in disconnecting myself from forces insisting I can't do without them, ones threatening to cut me off from the community of impersonal ties and power relations of which these forces assume me to be a part. I consider it a sign that they want me to stay too much for me to stay.

Psalm 84

"For a day in thy courts is better than a thousand. I had rather be a doorkeeper in the house of my God, than to dwell in the tents of wickedness." (Ps 84:10)

"I had rather be a doorkeeper in the house of God than to dwell in the tents of wickedness," writes the Psalmist. So would I. The problem is that while I do not consider myself integrated in the commercial society in which I live, this society does consider me integrated in it. It gives me no other option. Moreover, I have to pay to belong. This form of extortion entitles me to buy and use goods and to dispose of them after use to make room for other goods and their uses. The extent to which I choose to perpetuate this routine ensures my status as the most valuable commodity of all: homo consumers. I buy; therefore, I am.

Gifts once given freely by God are now considered inferior, repulsive, and degrading unless their market value can be established. People, too, are valuable only to the degree their buying habits match or exceed our own. More than thirty years ago, Richard Sennett warned of a new ideology of "shared interests" based on an "empathy for a select group of people allied in their rejection of those not within the local circle. Outsiders, unknowns, unlikes become creatures to be shunned."[1]

An *outsider* is anyone who in Zygmunt Bauman's description, attempts to live "the kind of life that reproduces itself without money changing hands."[2] What dawns on me is how hard it is to be an outsider even if one wants to—especially when practitioners of the market are doing all within their power to conquer areas of life not yet merchandized.

---

1. Sennett, "Cooperation."
2. Bauman, *Liquid Love*, 100.

Psalm 84

Yet, I think there may be a way. It involves scrutinizing what the market culture deems invaluable, then looking elsewhere. What they choose not to value, we should value, an approach that might be described as *via negativa*. In this way, we may still be able to find those places that flower in the desert. Of what variety are these flowers there? I suspect they'll bear a strong resemblance to poetry as yet published, songs as yet sung, and stories requiring the storyteller, above all, to be humble. The market won't know what to make of these because they are gifts of an untamable human spirit, seeming of little value. All we have to do is be careful not to advertise them.

Psalm 85

"Thou hast taken away all thy wrath: thou hast turned thyself from the fierceness of thine anger." (Ps 85:3)

We are currently involved in a war that is being rationalized and justified the way all wars are. This one happens to be run by the corporations for the benefit of the corporations. I would like not to have to worry about the situation, but that is impossible. People are dying, and the deeper we are into this thing, the less inclined the government will be able to get out of it. They'll talk about the need for increasing commitment, all the while serving the interests of mammon. They'll talk about the need for sacrifices while ensuring they make none of their own. And, finally, they'll invent a hideous, obscene language to keep us hopelessly optimistic, to narcotize us to the point of stupefaction so we won't notice the bodies piling up.

I am angry, so angry I'm trembling; I'm angry with the lies and liars who have no regard for life but only for profits. Increasingly, I feel like an expatriate in my own country. And, frankly, I don't want to hate the country's so-called leaders who currently hold us captive to their strategies. Like the Psalmist, I too am tempted to call down the wrath of God on them. In my heart of hearts, I want to see them suffer as much as they're going to make others suffer. It will not end soon. The air is poisoned all around.

Psalm 86

"O turn unto me, and have mercy upon me; give thy strength unto thy servant, and save the son of thine handmaid." (Ps 86:16)

At fifty, only someone in the throes of arrested development or adolescent addiction can refuse to acknowledge his or her own mortality. Consult an actuarial time line. Fifty is *not* middle age, a euphemism created to keep us from staring down an ever-narrowing corridor. This so-called middle age is nothing more nor less than the biological imperative that can be witnessed in the mirror. A person's face is one's own history.

As if that weren't enough, other startling indicators include the deaths of friends and colleagues, the overwhelming evidence of unfulfilled ambitions, and the gnawing suspicion that you've heard it all before. "The typical middle-aged individual," writes James Dickey, "has lost the sense of living life spontaneously, from the center of his being and his essential self, the real sense of the consequence of life. Indeed, as we grow older, everything tends to lose its sense of consequence and interest and vitality and grows tasteless, uninteresting, something to be endured."[1] I know of no better description of the desert of middle age in which I find myself now, walking in circles and drinking one too many brandies each evening.

I suppose one could say Dickey's dissection of the underbelly of middle age is cynical and despairing. I find hope in it because it provides the vision necessary for bringing one's priorities into sharp relief. At fifty, a person really has only two options. He or she can run headlong into fantasy, reviving the adolescent self, believing all the time in the world exists and that age is just a *state of mind*—commercial bromides and pseudo-mystical nonsense of the Chopra variety. Or an individual can continue on the quest, recognizing the stiff human cost incurred by those who attempt to

---

1. Powell, "James Dickey."

live authentically. Not everyone makes it. A survey of the human landscape reveals innumerable unearthed causalities. The desert can be merciless.

It is, however, the only place where getting lost offers the hope of being found. How was it Thoreau put it? He entered the wilderness to confront the essentials, attempting to discover what material possessions, necessities, he needed in order to live. What he found was a truth he wouldn't live without.[2] Only by forsaking false desires can we prepare ourselves for those possibilities flowering mercifully in the desert. I'm willing to wait for those as long as I can. The world has worn me out, and I'm tired of its many advertised satisfactions.

---

2. Thoreau, *Walden*, 3.

Psalm 87

"As well the singers as the players on instruments shall be there: all my springs are in thee." (Ps 87:7)

The spiritual warrior must be on guard for love's imposters. They abound and often go forth gathering converts in the name of God. Pushed to the wall and forced to give an account of themselves, they adopt the language of lawyers since control and power are their true objectives.

Those who would counterfeit love are generally of two types, just as Walker Percy points out in his novel *The Second Coming*. He calls them "believers who are intolerable" and "unbelievers who are insane," making the distinction clear in the following paragraph:

> And if the good news is true, why are its public proclaimers such assholes and the proclamation itself such a weary used up thing? . . . As unacceptable as believers are, unbelievers are even worse . . . [The unbeliever] is in fact an insane person . . . The present-day Christian is either half-assed, nominal, lukewarm, hypocritical, sinful, or, is fervent, generally offensive and fanatical. But he is not crazy. The present-day unbeliever is crazy as well as being an asshole—which is why I say he is a bigger asshole than the Christian because a crazy asshole is worse than a sane asshole. The rest of my life . . . shall be devoted to a search for the third alternative, a *tertium quid*—if there is one. If not we are stuck with two alternatives: (1) believers, who are intolerable, and (2) unbelievers who are insane.[1]

Percy makes it apparent that there are things he cannot live with, describing all too well the current religious and secular situations in this country. Unfortunately, when he wrote this book, he could not have anticipated to what extent the "believers, who are intolerable" would try to make

---

1. Percy, *Second Coming*, 190.

the rest of us believe the way they do, establishing a theocracy as repugnant and dangerous as the one inaugurated by the Puritans in seventeenth-century New England. If you know what people are supposed to believe, then you've already usurped God's authority, denying him the possibility of showing someone a different path, a *tertium quid*.

Even if we can't be sure of this path, we can be certain what it's not. It's not the confidence you are right and the subsequent sense you're entitled to chain another's soul. That circumstance is nothing more than spiritual fascism: the opposite of love. Maybe the solution to this dilemma is what Hannah Arendt calls a *refined atheism*, not the absence of belief displayed by unbelievers who are insane but a deepening of belief that comes from detaching ourselves from our own certain assumptions.[2] Why? Because a horrible kind of predestination hovers over our fixed notions of God until he too becomes another symptom of our everydayness, our ennui. We refuse him the freedom to live in us in unknowable and unbounded ways. Even our language traps him.

No better reason to cultivate an interior landscape, a place out of sight, where the word can be born and God is finally free to be himself without our help. Nor is there a need to convert anybody to anything since God's presence is all that matters. "My springs are in thee," he promises in the words of the Psalmist. What an extraordinary opportunity to live in the simplicity of newness and let others do the same. In this way we pose no obstacles to ourselves or anyone else on the path.

---

2. Arendt, "Atheism" (quoted in Bernard Magnus, *CCN*).

Psalm 88

"For my soul is full of troubles: and my life draweth nigh unto the grave." (Ps 88:3)

This psalm is almost a catalogue of the symptoms of classical depression. First, there is the sense that one is dying, that "my life draweth nigh unto the grave." This is not hyperbole. Anyone who has experienced this degree of depression knows that it is a full meltdown of the personality, leaving no self intact.

Then there is the admission that "I am as a man that hath no strength." People suffering from depression can't get out of bed. I mean that literally. It is as if something or someone is pinning you to the bed. You couldn't rise up if you wanted. Taking a bath or changing clothes requires an almost impossible expenditure of energy. Many of the homeless people we see wearing the same clothes do so because they're depressed.

Depression snatches a person out of the ordinary flux of life with separation from friends and family as an inseparable barrier: "Thou hast put away mine acquaintance far from me; thou hast made me an abomination to them." Family members wonder why the depressed individual doesn't just "shake it off." There seems to be something sinfully self-indulgent about depression that can't be said for cancer or heart disease. Depressed people put other people through hell, as well.

For this reason, the Psalmist proclaims that "I am counted with them that go down into the pit." Here "terrors have cut me off." True anxiety never knows its source. The feeling of abandonment is total: "Lord, why castest thou off my soul?" This is the definition of hell: separation from God.

For my own part, I've experienced serious depression twice. Both times something unexpected rose up from the subterranean depths of my childhood, slapping me hard. Both times I came to understand there was a fate worse than death, which is only to say I understand why some people don't make it. I'm glad I did. Having travelled through "the valley of the shadow of death," and come through it alive, I recognize the atmospheric facts of depression. In fact, the American Buddhist nun Pema Chodron describes it in those terms: "Depression is just like the weather—it comes and it goes. Lots of different feelings, emotions, and thoughts, they just come and go forever, but that's no reason to forget how precious life is."[1] If we can remember that, then the only appropriate response to life is gratitude.

Again, Pema Chodron offers us a considerable measure of help here:

> "When you find yourself with these old, familiar feelings of anxiety because your world is falling apart and you're not measuring up to your image of yourself and everybody is irritating you beyond words because no one is doing what you want and everyone is wrecking everything and you feel terrible about yourself and you don't like anybody else and your whole life is fraught with emotional misery and confusion and conflict, at that point just remember that you're going through all this upheaval because your coziness has just been, in some small way or large way, addressed. Basically, you *do* prefer life and warrior-ship to death."[2]

---

1. Chodron, *Awakening*, 189.
2. Chodron, *Awakening*, 190.

Psalm 89

"The days of his youth hast thou shortened: thou hast covered him with shame." (Ps 89:45)

I am not a prophet. I don't speak with authority. But I am a writer, and I try to honor the title by not being the sort of writer who panders to the trivial and sensational, to schlock and ignorance, writing books that end up being discussed on talk shows and collecting dust on coffee tables.

In short, my purpose is not to deliver the happy news or to write stories that are murderously sentimental, appealing to commercially sanctioned feelings that can be experienced for a price. In fact, much of what I write is in reaction to these pernicious manipulations. I am frequently motivated by rage. Despite what people think, being a writer is not romantic. On the contrary, it has, just as Walker Percy points out, its "own special miseries, which include isolation, madness, tics, amnesia, powers of speech."[1] The only thing worse than being a writer is being married to one.

Sometimes people (with the best of intentions, no doubt) ask me, "Wouldn't you be happier playing golf, watching football, driving an SUV, and drinking beer?"

"Probably," I say.

"Then why don't you?" they ask, faces brightening.

Although I have no pat answer, here's the one I'd offer if I did:

"As much as I appreciate your concern for me, I have chosen (or been chosen?) to be a writer, which is, perhaps, the loneliest and most anxiety-producing occupation in human history, with the possible exception of prophet. But even a prophet has God to talk to. There's never any doubt where the next inspiration is coming from. But writers are not so fortunate. If they take their work seriously, they have only one credential: trafficking

---

1. Percy, "Questions," 9–12.

in words and meanings. So the chronic misuse of words, especially the fobbing off of commercial slogans for truth, irks the writer. The wordsmith is aware too that such language blunts us to the atrocities of the age. For this reason, authentic writers must be proclaimers of banal atrocities—as much as people hate having these things pointed out."

Now add to this the whole business of the writer's being concerned with Christian preoccupations in an age when the language of Christianity has been degraded and rendered one big cliché, and you have one miserable person indeed. He or she might as well be sitting in the desert in sackcloth and ashes like contemporaries of old. But again, the author, despite the title, has not been given that authority. A scribe does the next best thing: attempting to remain sympathetic while being just ornery enough to get across the message that we're doing everything possible not to hear the good news. Like a yogi teetering atop a pole, the hapless writer surveys the landscape from an unsteady pinnacle and without the assurances of a prophet. It's extremely hard on the nerves.

Psalm 90

"So teach us to number our days that we may apply our hearts unto wisdom." (Ps 90:12)

A recent flu epidemic, surprising everyone by taking the life of a teenager here locally, reinforces the inefficacy of our vaccines and antibiotics to ensure that we will "be glad all our days." One of the themes of the Psalmist is the shortness of our time here; we are like grass which "flourisheth in the morning and in the evening is cut down and withereth." Our days are beset with troubles, as well. Our only hope is to look to the Lord for his loving kindness.

For some, this view seems embarrassingly quaint given the ability of our technology to subdue nature and to offer promises of a longer, more convenient life. We accept these promises on faith that someone, somewhere, knows what's best for us. We even begin to act as if the experts couldn't possibly be wrong. In our new technological utopia, death isn't feared; it isn't even noticed. We treat it as an alien and unnatural occurrence.

The Psalmist operates under no such delusion. His is not a question of whether, but of when. Thus, death's inevitability posits the terms by which we're expected to live. If death is trivialized or seen as meaningless, then so is life. This conundrum is inescapable, yet people on all fronts try to escape it.

Although understandable, this impulse results in sad consequences, sadder for not being seen as such. For instance, I know a man who recently took a job a thousand miles across the country. Both he and his wife agreed nothing should impede the man's career, so the wife will continue to work and live here while the husband will assume his new position in California. The couple is in their fifties. They have a seventeen-year-old daughter. They act as if they have all the time in the world.

By the same token, my wife and I met another couple recently who refuse to sleep more than three hours a night. "Sleep gets in the way of what we really want to be doing," the woman explained. "Besides, we're high-energy, career-minded people." They boast about their separate interests and about not needing to keep up with each other's whereabouts. "Sometimes he'll fly to Europe, and I won't even know he's going until he gets there and calls." This couple harbors the illusion that they maintain separate lives while being connected through technology. As such, they see no need to acknowledge good-byes, grief, loss, or death. Nor do they seek answers to questions of meaning since life is a problem that has already been solved. So what will their lives have signified to themselves and others? Irrelevant, given their ability to use the *delete* key on a computer.

A far cry from the Psalmist's assertion that all our life is preparation for dying, and that in dying we find out why it is we have lived. As for time and energy, only people in serious denial fail to realize that these things exist in limited quantities, gifts given to us for a while. What we do with them is "as a tale that is already told."

Psalm 91

"He that dwelleth in the secret place of the most High shall abide under the shadow of the Almighty." (Ps 91:1)

Given the insistence of so many little people willing to make themselves big gods, the Psalmist's voice offers a singular assurance: "He that dwelleth in the secret place of the most high shall abide under the shadow of the Almighty." The words beg to be repeated, piercing the fog and chasing away all shadows of a doubt that God will protect those of us who don't know who we are, only that we are lost. He will lead us into the desert because that is the special place he has prepared for us. We are never lost because he is always at our side: "He is my refuge and my fortress: My God in Him will I trust." I can have no better ally at my side; he chases away the ravening beasts—all the hatred and fears and figments that torment me and those around me: "Thou shalt not be afraid for the terror by night; nor for the arrow that flieth by day."

Only a God immune to the poisonous effects of evil can make such a promise. Of all the songs recited by the Psalmist, this one is no monody. The singer's voice blends into God's own, sure and true, flowing from one source. There is an almost imperceptible shift in syntax from the human to the divine: "Because he hath set his love upon me, therefore will I deliver him: I will set him on high, because he hath known my name." On high with God himself. The poem has come full circle with a promise gladly fulfilled: "With long life will I satisfy him and shed him my salvation."

Psalm 92

"To shew forth thy lovingkindness in the morning, and thy faithfulness every night." (Ps 92:2)

My son told me just the other day that he couldn't stand to listen to the radio any longer. He was referring to the various extremist media personalities who spew venom and excite old hatreds in the name of news and entertainment. "They made me sick—literally," he said. "I get a physical sensation of nausea whenever I hear them." I understand what he means. They are polluters of the soul, transmitting their words into the aether, confirming the notion that it is not what goes into a person, but what comes out of an individual that corrupts. Their abuse of the language and the spirit from which it derives is so frequent as to desensitize us to their routine atrocities. Therein lies the danger.

On any given day you can tune in and hear monotonously obscene rantings from speakers actually boasting that they're gods. As such, they have license to say and do all that mean and petty gods have done in the past. They taunt the weak and defenseless, justify their abusiveness with absurd platitudes and twisted thinking characteristic of psychotics, and target enemies for extinction. That's right. It's apparently okay to say that people who don't agree with your warped views should be killed.

The problem with shock media is that most people no longer find it shocking. It may even be mainstream given our collective paranoia and our need to stoke the embers of hatred so they don't go out. Millions listen each day in a country where six people out of every hundred thousand read an average of one book a year with *book* defined as a Harlequin romance or an action thriller. If books offer an occasion for reflection, extremist bombardment provides no such opportunity. Even the responses of callers are edited, culled deliberately, and selected strategically for their inanity

Psalm 92

and offensiveness. In such cases, it is always the shows' hosts who have the last word given the fascist nature of the medium and the messenger. Their words condemn them to a life of misery and ingratitude.

Not so our Psalmist. Not content merely to make noise, he listens in the silence of his heart for the word that belongs only to God and longs to be shared with others in gratitude. It is the word that shows forth "thy loving-kindness in the morning and thy faithfulness every night." It never makes demands or insists on being the final word. It is best heard as music: "Upon an instrument of ten strings and upon the psaltery; upon the harp with a solemn sound." Best of all, it imposes no burden for the rest of us to bear, that burden having already been borne by the broken heart of God.

Psalm 93

"The Lord on high is mightier than the noise of many waters, yea, than the mighty waves of the sea." (Ps 93:4)

How could God be like us and not have a broken heart? How could he not be crazy with worry and fear and love for the son who took his image? By its very nature, love requires us to be vulnerable. Ask any parent. Yet here the Psalmist clothes God in steel, girding him with impenetrable flesh. It is comforting to know God is strong. But it is comforting to know he is weak in ways that matter.

I have a friend whose son was killed in a car crash on his twenty-first birthday. He had red hair and a shy, arresting smile. He was good to small children—my son among them. His friends threw him a party. He had too much to drink and crashed late at night. I hate such ironies. They seem almost demonic.

What I recall most was the aura of suffering around his parents—a profound thing, as palpable as a force field warning people: "Stay back. What I have experienced is awful and terrible and beyond the power of words to tell." Their pain was in direct proportion to the amount of love they had for their son. What a brutal equation! Maybe the only one that matters.

Such love and suffering scare us to death, or maybe *unto* death would be a better way of putting it. For that reason, I understand the singer's desire to invoke the almighty, a god immune to the terrors of thermodynamics and the paradoxical claims of death. We're willing to try any stratagem that will keep those we love safe from harm. More power to the "Lord on high [who] is mightier than the noise of many waters." But there is also a place for a God who is driven mad by the excesses of love that require a miracle of understanding to comprehend.

Psalm 94

"How long shall they utter and speak hard things? and all the workers of iniquity boast themselves?" (Ps 94:4)

What happens when those "workers of iniquity boasting to themselves" claim to be in God's camp? Maybe if these people were a little less certain, a little more doubtful, professing their limitations and anxieties, there'd be some hope for us. As it is, I just don't know.

Who's to say God will intervene in matters of human will? There is no guarantee we will come to our senses, declaring war the most insidious illusion of all. Who was it who said that wars are religious? Why? Because everyone believes he or she alone possesses the truth. Our entire personalities are structured around this assumption.

But what would be the effect if one person actually took seriously the proposition: "Everything that I know is wrong"? I doubt that'll happen in a million years, or a million millennia, for that matter. Such honesty would force us to dismantle our carefully constructed self-images and the elaborately manufactured images of our nations too.

The most evil undertaking we can do is justify our hatreds in the name of God. Yet, who of us would not agree with Mark Twain when he says, "Man is a Religious Animal. Man is the only Religious Animal. He is the only animal that has the True Religion—several of them. He is the only animal that loves his neighbor as himself and cuts his throat if his theology isn't straight."?[1]

Even though the Psalmist assures us that the Lord who "formed the eye" sees the mischief done in his name, there's no assurance he will exact vengeance since that would only justify the aggression advocated by those

---

1. Twain, *Letters*, 36.

parading his cause. I do not believe God will give them that satisfaction. It is up to us to set a different example. Therein lies our hope.

Until the fruits of that hope are harvested, we will be forced to endure the alarming spectacle of so-called people of God and influence who make public statements as the following:

> "You say you're supposed to be nice to the Episcopalians and the Presbyterians and the Methodists and this, that, and the other thing. Nonsense. I don't have to be nice to the spirit of the Antichrist."

> "The feminist agenda is not about equal rights for women. It is about a socialist, anti-family political movement that encourages women to leave their husbands, kill their children, practice witchcraft, destroy capitalism, and become lesbians."

> "Our goal is a Christian nation. We have a biblical duty, we are called by God to conquer this country. We don't want equal time. We don't want pluralism."

I won't dignify the authors by revealing their identities. They are well-known ministers in the public eye. What I will say is that their rants sound more like the screeds of the Third Reich rather than the good news of Jesus. They don't seem to grasp that it isn't God who judges us, but we ourselves. Sadly, we're all living reminders of a Yiddish proverb: "A man's worst enemies can't wish on him what he can think up for himself."

Psalm 95

"O come, let us sing unto the LORD: let us make a joyful noise to the rock of our salvation." (Ps 95:1)

A grateful heart is a good thing. We have a need to feel grateful. Though I've never read it in any of the psychoanalytic literature, it wouldn't surprise me if gratitude isn't a requirement for being an emotionally healthy person. Of course, I'm not defining gratitude as duty—the obligation we feel to tick off all the blessings we can recall at Thanksgiving.

I'm talking about an unexpected outpouring of the heart, an epiphany, a revelation, that I am suddenly at one with the natural world in ways I never knew before. Today, it is a patch of snow on my deck out back. In a few hours, it will be gone. But here it is now on this bright, sharp, clear, cold Sunday morning sprawled like a still-sleeping spirit just feet away, not ready yet to evaporate, to be called heavenward. I am grateful for its oneness and the miracle of its lingering. Like me, it will readily go back to its source. We are given a day to shine in gratitude, the Psalmist reminds us. I will gratefully take the memory of this patch of snow with me everywhere I go today.

Psalm 96

"For all the gods of the nations are idols: but the LORD made the heavens." (Ps 96:5)

The false gods of materialism and ambition are everywhere to be found. And make no mistake. They are gods, requiring our time, energy, and devotion. The more of these gods we own, the more they own us, the more they consume us and displace a devotion that rightly belongs to God.

Poverty is the true state of humankind. I don't mean the abject state forcing people to do without the essentials of housing, goods, clothing, and healthcare. I mean the emptiness of intention that makes room for God and no other. To be empty of the desires of this world is the first step in acknowledging that God is not required to compete with all the petty gods of our own creation. He reigns, indivisible.

One of the most unsettling of new trends in conspicuous consumption is for parents to throw obscenely lavish "Sweet Sixteen" parties for their daughters. A wealthy San Antonio, Texas, couple threw their teenaged daughter a six-million-dollar bash for the girl and six hundred of her friends. The celebration took place in a fifty-five thousand square-foot venue decorated with thirty-foot tall cherry trees. The parents said of the event that they wanted to give their "princess" an unforgettable experience to make her transition into adulthood. One can only wonder how this child will ever develop realistic expectations putting her on equal footing with the mass of humanity.

An overly indulgent mom in Knoxville, Tennessee, hosted an over-the-top "Sweet Fifteen" extravaganza for her daughter costing more than two million. The girl's mother forked over thousands in pricey designer gowns, hairdressers, and make-up artists for her daughter's "princess" court of friends, and a dance troupe and a rapper from Georgia who provided entertainment. The teen also received a special-edition BMW valued at fifty thousand. When criticized in the local press for spending an amount that could feed a third-world country, the mother replied, "It's my money. I'll do what I want with it." As it turned out, the money wasn't hers. The lavish event attracted federal investigators curious how a bookkeeper for a brokerage firm could acquire such wealth. The answer: embezzlement to the tune of more than four million dollars. At times, it would seem, hubris has its consequences.

I have thought often what sort of adults these spoiled and pampered children become. Do they stand a chance of acquiring compassion, empathy, and selflessness, or are they doomed to fulfill the narcissistic expectations of a culture valuing wealth and celebrity above the operations of soul making?

Psalm 97

"For thou, LORD, art high above all the earth: thou art exalted far above all gods." (Ps 97:9)

The Psalmist is forever trying to appease the omnipotent God of the desert. It is a superstitious overture as old as humans themselves. How to tame the untamable? How to diminish the certainty of God's wrath? The fact that the Psalmist spends so much time attesting to God's strength only serves to expose the shadow of our weakness. Why on Earth then is Yahweh described as a jealous god when all the odds are in his favor? He can smite any time he wants, never being forced to explain himself.

In the absence of the grossest sentimentality, what we secretly know is that the human condition is inordinately unfair. The cards are stacked against us from the first. We are born in trouble and die in trouble, and in between we act with insufficient knowledge. Consider the child who chases a ball into the street only to be struck and killed by a car. One mistake and it's over. That's the precariousness of life. Anyone who thinks otherwise is bedeviled by serious delusions.

The novelist Ann Goethe has an arresting passage in her book *Midnight Lemonade* that sums it up. She's describing all the superstitions a mother is willing to entertain. As her protagonist confesses, "I have set spells, made vows, and kept bargains for the lives of my children."[1] There's the crux of it: the joy of having children, the unfathomable horror of losing them. Upon observing a child sleeping in a cradle, Pascal remarked, "Here lies God's competition."[2] The philosopher was acknowledging the unjust power of God not to have to suffer the most horrible of human fates. Indeed, all our skulking and bowing before God is a ruse designed to disguise

---

1. Goethe, *Midnight Lemonade*, 4.
2. Pascal, *Internet Encyclopedia*.

our contempt and hatred of him, appeasing him in the hope that he would sacrifice someone else's child and not our own. Look at the blood-lusting God of the Old Testament, of Abraham and Isaac, and the terrors of the sacrificed children, their cries unheard.

Reaching into the inarticulate unconsciousness of his people, God unearthed the bitter fruit he himself could never taste: the life-in-death, death-in-life paradox that makes us mad with desire that he should suffer too. At that point, it was as if he asked, "What can I do to banish the distance between us?" It was as if we replied, "We want your heart to break just like ours. If your love is authentic, you'll come down from your high station and submit to the ultimate sacrifice, the loss of a human child." So he did.

Jesus entered this veil of terrors and chaos without any of the divine privileges that were his birthright. Like us, he knew what it was like each evening to watch the sun sink from view, leaving marooned mankind behind. Like us, he had to act with insufficient knowledge, trembling with the awful awareness that the human condition is itself a state of being ultimately abandoned. Seen from this view, the phrase "He humbled himself" takes on hitherto unknown meaning.

It is no wonder the Bible tells us that the earth quaked and the rocks rent at the instant of Jesus's death. It was the beginning and the end of God's life as we conceive it. The splitting of the veil in the temple, no mere metaphor, was a sign that the distance between the human and the divine had dissolved for all time. At last we were one, made whole again by the love-in-death actions of Jesus. God's broken heart poured forth an inexhaustible wellspring of love. Love for the son was the same love God has for us. No difference. All the Christological categories so troubling us today were reconciled on the cross. Jesus as savior, brother, friend, son of God, redeemer—all apply. All are insignificant before the source and fact of love.

Psalm 98

"O sing unto the Lord a new song; for he hath done marvelous things: his right hand, and his holy arm, hath gotten him the victory." (Ps 98:1)

Many of the psalms exult in urging us to "sing unto the Lord a new song." Peaks and troughs, hills and valleys—the psalms reflect the oscillatory nature of the human quest, the ups and downs of our emotional and spiritual life. The truth is that we do not always feel like praising God. The way some people bandy his name about makes us reluctant ever to hear him mentioned again. Let us find him in silence, away from all talk of religion. It is the religionists, often the professional ones, who crucify him without knowing or caring, mistaking their vocation for their salvation.

Praising the Lord should never be a tired task. Nor should we be driven like quarry slaves to do it. When coerced, praise produces a hollow note rather than a new song.

I suppose the older we get, the harder it is to find such novelty. The desert is drier, and we have heard many of the same songs before. Voices, even beloved ones, begin to drone, and we're inclined to finish people's sentences for them. Why? We've heard their monodies already. People are predictable precisely because they sing old songs. How God must get tired of hearing us!

Knowing when not to praise may be the greatest praise of all. A silent heart may perceive new sounds. Just this morning I heard a crow calling outside on my lawn. It put me in the mind of my father who could call crows close by making a shrill sound that elicited peals of laughter from me as a child. I can't duplicate my father's crow call, but I can hear it in memory, and I heard it again this morning in praise of all he and I once shared. If so inclined, I'll hold that song close for the rest of the day, not giving it a name for fear of losing it.

Psalm 99

"The LORD reigneth; let the people tremble: he sitteth between the cherubims; let the earth be moved." (Ps 99:1)

Let there be no doubt. God is a warrior. As disturbing and distasteful as we may find it, the Psalmist declares that people "tremble" in God's presence. Even in the act of forgiving his people, God is not beyond taking "vengeance on their intentions." This paradox in God's nature most of us would as soon not face.

Yet I know of no one who wants an abstract, intellectualized form of protection when faced with a very real and muscular evil. Contrary to what some enlightened people believe, evil is not merely a projection. Jesus himself worried that the Evil One was on the prowl in search of innocents, those whose goodness offered little protection against the minions of terror and the jackboots of brutality. Even now people are being raped or molested or killed. They need protection, not abstract philosophy. They require a warrior God to save them from unspeakable horrors.

The Israelites counted on such a God. It is true that evil resides within, but it also resides without. The ancient Hebrews faced objective enemies that threatened them with extinction. They knew first-hand what Ambrose Redmoon expressed when he says:

> There are those with a clear conscience and immense power who enjoy the full exercise of their will at the expense of others. Sadistic greed is combined with a clear, intelligent mind and a tough, powerful, fast physique, all in a person who is quite beyond the reach of 'consciousness lifting.' Such people are not confused, they are not victims, they are not seeking. They are not cowards, most

of them. They are going to abuse, terrify, and possess because they find it efficient and enjoyable.[1]

To let them have their way is both masochistic and sinful. It is true Jesus tells us to turn the other cheek. But we submit to the worst form of literalism if we fail to embrace the paradox that Jesus himself was a warrior, placing himself between innocence and evil, forcing the Devil to overplay his hand while giving Jesus all the power he needed to wage battle for the souls of his beloved ones.

With fear and trembling, we ought to pray, "Lead us not into temptation but deliver us from evil." Everyday each of us should tremble in hopes of not contributing to the horrific evils afoot in the world. Neither should we regard it as contradiction when we are required to use all within our power to stop bullies, whether they be people, institutions, even nations (including our own) from violating the innocent, weak, and vulnerable. If you have it in mind to do harm to "the least of these," then consider the terrible price of discovering that the victimizer may be a victim begging to be stopped. Consider, too, the soul's injury to that person whose remotest desire, but only option, is to stop him.

---

1. Redmoon, "No Peaceful Warriors," 40–45.

Psalm 100

"Make a joyful noise unto the LORD, all ye lands." (Ps 100:1)

We exist on the canvas of God's imagination, which is another way of saying we have no existence apart from God. We cannot conceive of a single idea beyond what God has already conceived of. We are *in* him in every possible way. His love for us is the fact of our creation. For this reason, the Bible tells us that we are made in His image. Because He is love, we are made in love, never to be separated from the source of our being.

As a child I awoke to the moment and mystery of my existence. There was a time when I was not. Then I was—with only tender memories of the few days I had been. Without a history I lay in the grass, losing all thought of myself in the deep blue throat of the sky. The wind whispered its thoughts to me. I held up my hand, examining it in wonder.

Wonder is a form of wordless praise. It is a silent song that offers thanksgiving. Giving thanks is the recognition of our inseparable relationship with a God whose ways are unknowable, whose beginning and end start at a point and proceed in opposite directions in a paradox of timelessness. Once upon a time is all time for God. His story, one that includes us, is everlasting in the wonder it evokes. We are as mysterious and sacred as the God who makes us. Standing in this mystery finds me at a flashpoint of joy that remains nameless to this day. Only by being unknown to myself am I known as God's own.

Psalm 101

"I will sing of mercy and judgment: unto thee, O LORD, will I sing."
(Ps 101:1)

I had a medical procedure yesterday, the results of which, had they been different, could have spelled serious trouble. I couldn't help thinking someone received the bad news I was spared. What does it mean to be "spared," after all? The idea conjured up an image of God I refuse to accept: One who spares some while inflicting others. Why was I spared a death sentence and not someone else? Was it because of my intrinsic worthiness and someone else's corresponding unworthiness? Hardly. Was it because God needs me to do what no one else can? Am I that indispensable? The notion is laughably absurd. All my charms and spells and petitions about the reasonableness of leaving me here could not budge God an inch if he wasn't already inclined.

Yet, make no mistake. I prayed that the cup containing the dregs of sorrow and death pass from me. Here's my not-so-secret confession: I would let Jesus drink the cup for me. I would let him bear the burden of my desire to live at his expense. It doesn't take a sage to see what he has borne for me already or how many times I have been spared the sorrow he's accepted. It is only right that I give him thanks and praise, inhaling his sacrifices with my every breath.

We are at the cornerstone of all paradox now. For if the law of the universe is sacrifice, then yesterday someone worthier than I received the death sentence intended for me. Why was I spared? Not because I was worthy, but because he, in all his mercy, granted me reprieve. The thought alone should make us shiver: No matter what our appointed time, he's walked before us, in the same steps we would have taken all alone.

Psalm 102

"My days are like a shadow that declineth; and I am withered like grass." (Ps 102:11)

We live in the shadow of our failures. Even at our best and most aware, we are imprisoned as selves in time, capable of being only who and what we are at a given moment. This circumstance is at the heart of all our regrets.

Yesterday my wife and I were driving the road that curves toward our home, each of us noticing the stark outline and features of the winter's day. Newness in old things makes them precious to us: sycamores white as bones, horses, their sleek necks bent to the ground, grazing dreamily.

"My heart is smitten" with such scenes and the feelings that attend them. The odd mix of melancholy and memory reminds us how quickly our days are "consumed." Like a photograph album in the mind's eye, I recalled the now unrecallable past, saying to my wife, "I wish I was young and strong again and had a *small* boy to raise." Not that we aren't proud of the young man our son has become. We certainly love him no less or want to halt the time that gives him a history of his own. "It's just that—" I paused, my wife, mercifully completing my thought: "It's just that life is unfolding. And though we've always known that, we're living it now." I could scarcely bear the weight of our lives at that moment or fathom all the half-hearted choices that suddenly seemed ominous. Yet, there it was too the undeniable joy of a life lived, its ending mercifully predictable, if for no other reason than the assurance the Psalmist offers about his God: "But thou art the same, and thy years have no end."

Psalm 103

"As for man, his days are as grass: as a flower of the field, so he flourisheth." (Ps 103:15)

This psalm is a lengthy lament about the shortness of our time here: "As for man, his days are as grass: as a flower in the field, so he flourisheth. For the wind passeth over it, and it is gone; and the place thereof shall know it no more." The beauty of dissolution is heard in the way the lines whisper our fate.

Juxtaposed to life's brevity, however, is the "everlasting mercy" of the Lord, merciful in part, because it *is* eternal, forgiving, redeeming, and satisfying, "so that thy youth is renewed like the eagle's." Unless we plumb a little deeper, this last phrase will ring hollow, offering hope that the energies and direction of the psalm quickly extinguish, that is, unless we consider what it means to be youthful. Youth is a time of vulnerability. Most of us recall the panic of being small, faced with circumstances new and overwhelming. I'm not sure we ever rid ourselves of the primal fears lurking in the dark corners of our past. We cling to the memory of those who offered us protection at a crucial time. It we were lucky, this person was a parent, a father or mother mad with love for us.

Yet, we also know that parents can be a disappointing species. They grow old and weak, and then they die. Still, they are our first exposure to a power that is almost godlike. That is why it is only natural for the Psalmist to draw this comparison, by saying, "Like a father pitieth his children, so the Lord pitieth them that [love] him." This statement assumes much. It assumes that fathers are loving and good. It assumes they will not foist their failures, shame, unfulfilled hopes, and frustrated ambitions on their children. What emerges here is an archetype of the perfect father. As we all know, there are no perfect human fathers—or mothers either, though the latter tend to be idealized more than the former.

But the Psalmist is trying to give us a touchstone in ordinary experience for understanding God's love. Because we are human, we are made with the divine image in us. Thus, we can't help loving, despite ourselves at times. Not even in hell can we escape the influence of love. The imperfect love of fathers then points to the perfect love of the one true Father.

In his poem "Those Winter Sundays," Robert Hayden tells about growing up in a house plagued with "chronic angers." He acknowledges that he held little affection for his father, though the man rose every day, putting on his clothes on in the "blueblack cold"[1] and "then with cracked hands that ached / from labor in the weekday weather made / banked fires blaze."[2] The final verdict on this scene: "No one ever thanked him."[3] Everything we need to know about failed love and regret can be found in this line. Not one of us escapes the imperfection of our humanity or our need for a perfect father. Even when sacrifice flowers in our midst, there's no guarantee we'll grasp the nature of the gift we're receiving: "What did I know, what did I know / of love's austere and lonely offices?"[4]

---

1. Hayden, "Those Winter," 2.
2. Hayden, "Those Winter," 3–5.
3. Hayden, "Those Winter," 5.
4. Hayden, "Those Winter," 13–14.

Psalm 104

"He causeth the grass to grow for the cattle, and herb for the service of man: that he may bring forth food out of the earth." (Ps 104:14)

One particularly offensive "conservative" journalist made a statement recently in an effort to justify destroying public lands: "God says, the Earth is yours. Take it. Rape it. It's yours." Fortunately, the Psalmist's hymn of praise offers an antidote to such poisonous violence, countering the columnist's appalling ignorance by reminding us that the Earth is anything but ours. We neither created it, nor will we be able to do anything but return to it once our time is over. We own nothing—not even our lives.

The Psalmist further reminds us of our creatureliness by describing all the non-human joys experienced by other creatures with whom we share the Earth as a gift. Their presence should delight our hearts rather than inflame our insane aggression toward them because they are unlike us. If God cares about them, why shouldn't we? After all, "He causeth the grass to grow for the cattle" and he instills the instinct by which "the birds make their nests." God even adjusts the light for the convenience of "the least of these": "Thou makest darkness, and it is night wherein all the beasts of the forests do creep forth." Is it any wonder our Lord chose a stable where he could surround himself with his favorites at the time of his birth? Such a scene ought to give us an abiding sense of our place in the divine scheme. To be human is a privilege. Even the origin of the word *human* shares the same etymological root as *humility* and *humus*, the latter meaning soil.

Psalm 105

"Seek the LORD, and his strength: seek his face evermore." (Ps 105:4)

As a people in captivity, the Israelites vacillate between offering God praise for past victories and decrying his ability to provide similar victories now. Such is the nature of the spiritual journey: evidence of God's presence followed by fear of his absence. Faith is posited in doubt and, often, in stark terror.

We can be captive to our own urges. Following these urges lets us cling to the comfort and security of familiar patterns, bad as they may be for us. A known evil is better than an unknown one. As every alcoholic knows, no one wants to enter the dark forest without a good stiff drink first, something to deaden us to the reality of the uncertain journey ahead. Compulsions are old friends, after all. They help alleviate anxiety. We enshrine them as good angels wooing us to safe harbors. In reality, they are sirens threatening our soul's progress, keeping us from our appointed task of making sure the journey doesn't go stale.

To that end, the Psalmist is our spiritual guide, telling us to seek the "face" of God. It's an oddly anthropomorphic image since most of us identify God as spirit. Its full implications can be gleaned only when we consider who it is who wears the face of God. Jesus is the visible image of the Deity. His human form reveals his divine nature. Consider the tear-streaked face of Jesus weeping for his friend Lazarus. Imagine Jesus's hands—their lifelines pierced with spikes. From a distance, witness the stoop of his shoulders as he touched and healed the crowd. Tremble at his furious visage, all the more so for normally being patient and kind, when the money-lenders sought to make a mockery of the sacred place. The face of God is all around us, witnessing our captivity with enough sympathy to break a human heart and enough love to help us to our feet, promising to be our companion till we arrive safely home.

Psalm 106

"And he saved them from the hand of him that hated them, and redeemed them from the hand of the enemy." (Ps 106:10)

This psalm is a poignant recapitulation of all the times God "redeemed [his people] from the enemy." It recalls the Israelites' escape from Egypt and the way the Lord caused the waters to close round the pursuing army in the midst of the Red Sea. In short, it is a beautifully drawn and dramatic account. No wonder Hollywood has lent it epic proportions.

But it is more than that. Here the Psalmist outlines an archetypal human predicament, one, nonetheless, reinforcing the inseparable knot tying us to God. The stages of this predicament can be summarized as follows: crisis, confession, salvation, lapse, punishment (self-inflicted), and redemption by God. In historical terms, the ancient people of the Lord found themselves needing to be rescued. As a result, God intervenes, dispatching them to safety. He "regards their affliction" and hears their cries. However, it doesn't take Yahweh's chosen ones long to forget Him. A lapse in spirituality is often a lapse in memory. Indeed, forgetting God results in a self-imposed captivity far worse than the servitude demanded by an enemy: "And they served their idols: which were a snare unto them. Yea, they sacrificed their sons and daughters unto devils, and shed innocent blood, even the blood of their sons and of their daughters, whom they sacrificed unto the idols of Canaan: and the land was polluted with blood. Thus, they were defiled with their own works, and went a whoring with their own intentions." Here the Psalmist alludes to the abominable practice of sacrificing children to the Canaanite deity, Moloch.

Slaying children as a way of appeasing bloodthirsty gods was a common practice in the ancient world. Here is the crucial difference: the one true God demands no such sacrifices. Indeed, it is he who will sacrifice on our behalf. He has the last word, and that word made flesh is one saving us despite our best efforts not to be saved. Forgetting God may be the source of all our misery and mischief. But he will not let us forget him for long. It is not our wish to repent that preserves us from our own worst excesses, but God's patience and long-suffering that woo our souls back to him and his love. He wants nothing more than that. He seeks no sacrifice other than that we quit sacrificing ourselves to those gods of our own making that result in our destruction. As for reminders, we seem to require them on a regular basis: "And He remembered for them His covenant and repented according to the multitude of His mercies."

Psalm 107

"He poureth contempt upon princes, and causeth them to wander in the wilderness, where there is no way." (Ps 107:40)

According to a book by a professor of Economic Development at the Carnegie Mellon Institute, a new "creative class" now exists in America. This jargon is receiving much currency at present, as cities brainstorm ways to attract members of this class who represent the artistic-scientific-consumerist princes of the age.[1] These are the folks who presumably will transform "wilderness" into a "fruitful land." If I am singularly unconvinced, it's because I recognize when desperate hopes are being packaged for consumption.

Who are these new princes? They are young, technologically savvy nomads not given to staying in one place or job for long. In fact, over a five-year period, they're likely to switch jobs an average of 3.5 times. For this reason, they're encouraged to have "weak ties," defined largely as "helpful acquaintances" rather than friends or family since the latter tend to tie one down, promoting unnecessary obligations. The new creative class needs their freedom; they wear what they want at work, and "body art" is one desirable form of their self-expression.

Work too, is fluid, more concept than actuality. If they work at an office at all, the ambience is Bohemian (i.e., Everyone "owns" a view), and no one keeps track of the hours though everyone suffers from "time famine." Gathering places are common as people discuss music or a new play while sipping chilled white wine at a designated oasis, nothing too deep or serious because next week you may find yourself in Seattle.

As best I can tell, this new elite scorns making or doing anything. If you have to ask what they do, then you've missed the point. It's enough to be

---

1. Florida, *Rise*, 1–208.

a poem. You don't have to write one. What is this group's vision of an ideal work situation? Making a lot of money while helping the poor via distance delivery on the web. If you've figured out by now that the creative class is a corporate marketing phenomenon designed to inflate egos and to give the appearance of infinite variety, then you're well on your way to discovering the underbelly of this arrangement: The global economy promotes loyalty to no one. In an age of "weak ties," everyone is on his or her own, no matter how we try to package the appeals.

Not long ago, I came across a wonderful definition of *delusion*: "Delusion is a vivid false belief, often felt by its victim to be threatening or exciting, and often associated with psychotic states. Normally sane people can suffer delusions when caught up in group hysteria." In other words, it is one thing to be foolish! It is another thing to believe one's foolishness. Perhaps the most serious delusion of all is believing we can remake ourselves on a daily basis—the postmodern fantasy that we aren't required to have a history or to be responsible for our actions. All we have to do, it seems, is offer an image for public consumption. The more we alter this image, making it ever newer, the more tragically delusional we become. For even people who make their own laws for their own circumstances—sometimes on the spot—don't always find the desert an easy place with so many parched souls there.

America has always been expert at spawning fads and recycling them later in a new package. The success of these enterprises requires sleight of hand and misdirection and total buy-in by participants necessary to sustain the illusion. I've no doubt that new creative class will be a thing of the past before long and that whatever replaces it will be embraced with an equally tiresome frenzy.

Psalm 108

"O God, my heart is fixed: I will sing and give praise, even with my glory." (Ps 108:1)

There has always been a priestly class of people whose hearts are "fixed" on the Lord. They don't necessarily wear collars or profess vows, but they sometimes find themselves in opposition to those who do. When genuine spirituality is missing, religion seeks to assert itself. All too often, the result is spiritual death, the emptying of authentic content and the freezing of it in formulas. All that's left are meaningless symbols and hollow slogans.

Walker Percy observed more than sixty years ago that the language of Christianity was worn out. It was so abused, misused, and commodified, he said, as to fail to signify, to point to any underlying reality.[1] Let's assume the situation is worse now than when Percy was writing if for no other reason than the information technologies and an increasing commodification of all areas of life can't help but transform religion, as well. When the church allies itself with business and political interests, it soon becomes indistinguishable from those interests, exploiting its own deeply treasured religious symbols, images, and stories, while participating in its own destruction. St. Augustine warned about the "stench of commerce" and how it lingers long after the initial transaction is completed.[2]

Yet, the transactions multiply. According to Michael Buddle and Robert Brimlow, two writers who keep track of such trends, the Pontiff in modern times is the world's most desirable product endorser: "His image is used to promote cement companies and bakeries, and to sell music CDs, videotapes, t-shirts, hats, mugs, and potato chips. His tours attract

---

1. Percy, *Message*, 101–118.
2. Augustine, *Confessions*, 117.

corporate sponsors, such as Federal Express, Mercedes Benz, Kodak, Hewlett Packard, and Pepsi."[3]

An alliance with such for-profit culture industries would seem to make it difficult for the church to criticize or censure corporate practices that exploit the poor. Even more disturbing, perhaps, is the way market-driven approaches have invaded religious education programs, encouraging educators and parents to remind children not to feel guilty for having money or enjoying things. So much for Jesus's kinship with the poor or his recognition that "the foxes have holes, and the birds of the air have nests; but the Son of man hath not where to lay his head."[4]

Even more to the point, Jesus scolds the Pharisees for profiteering in the Lord's house: "Ye fools and blind: for whether is greater, the gold, or the temple, that sanctifieth the gold?"[5] Jesus' stern admonition reminds us how crucial it is to value spiritual blessings over material ones and how quickly the Good News can become a market-laden message making it nearly impossible to glorify God "above all the earth."

---

3. Budde and Brimlow, *Christianity Inc.*, 73.
4. Matt 8:20.
5. Matt 23:17.

Psalm 109

"Let them be before the LORD continually, that he may cut off the memory of them from the earth." (Ps 109:15)

The Psalmist's enemy has cursed him. Therefore, the Psalmist wants his enemy to be cursed. So ferocious is his desire for revenge that, in a fit of pique, he spews forth a hellish sentence for the man, not realizing that their fates are intertwined and reciprocal:

> Let his days be few; and let another take his office.
> Let his children be fatherless, and his wife a widow.
> Let his children be continually vagabonds, and beg: let them seek their bread also out of their desolate places.
> Let the extortioner catch all that he hath; and let the strangers spoil his labor.
> Let there be none to extend mercy unto him: neither let there be any to favour his fatherless children.

The most extreme course of all, however, brings, God into the act: "Let him be before the Lord continually, that his memory may be removed from the earth." There isn't one of us who hasn't felt such rage or entertained such spite, if only temporarily. The human imagination knows few limitations in devising systematic tortures for those perceived to be enemies. This fact alone underscores John Milton's assertion that "the mind is its own place, and in it self / Can make a heav'n of hell, a hell of heav'n."[1] Hell is not what we wish for our enemies but what we insist on keeping for ourselves when we nurse grudges and re-enact episodes of injustice. These hurts amount to self-inflicted wounds.

It should go without saying that I cannot curse someone without cursing myself. Our destinies become inextricably connected. Yet, the Psalmist

---

1. Milton, *Paradise Lost*.

here agrees to be an unwitting accomplice in his own demise, giving his energy, his very soul, to a self-defeating quest for revenge. The battle is over before it starts.

Jesus understood all too well this human tendency. That is why he offered the following solution to our collective predicament: "Ye have heard that it that been said, Thou shalt love thy neighbor, and hate thine enemy. But I say unto you, love your enemies, bless them that curse you, do good to them that hate you, and pray for them which despitefully use you, and persecute you."

An absurd proposition? Not when we consider that Jesus is giving us a key designed to unlock the door to the only hell: the one we create for ourselves. What is it Mephistopheles says in Marlowe's *Faustus*? "Why, this is hell, nor am I out of it."[2] Jesus also echoes an observation made by Lao-tzu five hundred years earlier:

> For every force there is a counterforce.
> Violence, even well intentioned, always rebounds upon oneself.[3]

---

2. Marlowe, *Faustus*, 190.
3. Lao Tzu, "Violence."

Psalm 110

"The Lord at thy right hand shall strike through kings in the day of his wrath." (Ps 110:5)

Narcissism is apparently a requirement of the age. Witness the cult of celebrity, our contemporary form of idol worship. Indeed, the worst fate a person can experience is to be anonymous. This anonymity leads people to posture and pretend they're anything but who they are. Self-advertising knows no limits.

Odd, that. I know it's been some time ago; but when I was a child, I heard countless warnings about the evils of boasting. "Let someone else tout your accomplishments" was the caveat of conventional wisdom. A person could have numerous accomplishments; he or she just wasn't supposed to talk about them. In my neighborhood a braggart was subject to ridicule and scorn. What we respected was a person who could do exceptional things without fanfare. It's what the Italians call *sprezzatura*.

My hero back then was a boy named Greg Sessoms, five years my senior. I believe I respected Greg because he had the courage not to prove how courageous he was at every opportunity. I've seen him walk away from a fight without a trace of fear on his face. Yet, let someone pick on one of us younger or smaller boys, and Greg would show up as if on cue, never backing down. At that point, whoever was doing the bullying often had hell to pay. Greg believed in fairness, and in the best tradition of the Miles Chirstianus, the spiritual warrior, he defended the weak and those otherwise relegated to the fringes. He never bothered competing or comparing, unnecessary activities when one knows oneself. As unusual as it may sound, he couldn't have been more than fourteen or fifteen-years-old at the time.

That self-knowledge is hard to come by in an age when people are busy promoting themselves. Next month, I'm required to submit a self-evaluation to my department head. She will expect it to contain all of my past year's accomplishments with a bit of hyperbole thrown in for good measure. A far cry from the "good works" mentioned in Scripture, those acts of kindness and love that flourish best when hidden from view. In so many words, Jesus never ceases to remind us: Charity loses count of its own accord.

Psalm 111

"They stand fast for ever and ever, and are done in truth and uprightness."
(Ps 111:8)

After arriving home from work the other day, my wife related the plight of a young girl named Sara, the daughter of a good friend. It seems Sara received a sporty work-out suit for Christmas. Proud of it, she decided to wear it to school.

Sara is naturally athletic, a gifted basketball and soccer player. Nevertheless, on seeing her in her new outfit, some kids started taunting her, calling her a "lesbian," a stereotype often perpetuated by the image reinforced in school yards and in the media. Female athletes have always had a hard time of it, and Sara's schoolmates were relentless in their hazing of her. While conveying the incident to her mother, Sara burst into tears, but not before saying how she'd tried to do what Christ would do, not responding in kind but turning the other cheek. I know this young girl and do not doubt it one bit.

It says much about us as a society that we are all too indifferent to such episodes, seeing them, in such cases, as nothing more than rites of passage, leaving no lasting effects. I do not believe that to be the case. What I suspect is that people among us are placed here to help us. They enter this life in the usual manner, but they are different in ways that matter. Maybe they have an innate innocence about them, a light in the eyes that can't be extinguished. They are willing to be compassionate and aware, qualities that make them susceptible to being victimized by those with coarser sensibilities, those who have not yet awakened to their spiritual journey and are afraid to embark on that venture.

Sara stood her ground, but at what price to her young spirit? Someone might say she was building spiritual muscle. Perhaps. But how many other kids fail to survive the isolation and cruelty we've come to accept as status quo? The other day I read about a thirteen-year-old Maine youth who hanged himself after months of teasing by his classmates. What if his "differences" were those of someone with a more refined sensibility and higher level of awareness? What if he'd been placed here to teach us something indispensable about ourselves? We'll never know what that was, or in what ways this young man may have died for our sins.

Every human story is sacred. Until we learn that, I can only tremble at the thought of the damage we do. It's an odd propensity we have to damn ourselves. No one else does it for us. I only pray that no more causalities are required for us to see all the ways we crucify the human likeness of Christ.

Psalm 112

"He shall not be afraid of evil tidings: his heart is fixed, trusting in the LORD." (Ps 112:7)

The Psalmist leaves no doubt about the qualities of a good person. They're the same ones that belong to God: "He [or she] is gracious and full of compassion." Who wants to arrive at the end of life and not have learned these graces? Anything else we deem important is simply an illusion.

We are not only beneficiaries of grace and compassion; we are the agents through which these qualities find expression in the world. We are the divine representatives of a goodness that doesn't begin or end with us.

The enemy to all goodness is fear. Fear divides humanity into camps of *us* versus *them*. The resulting mischief has an estimable impact on all areas of life, causing us to develop strategies for dealing with our "enemies." The workplace is often an arena for such warring practices. People identify enemies and create alliances in order to protect themselves. From whom and what are we seeking protection? From people like ourselves and behavior like our own. In short, we collude with the Enemy in our own demise. Is any of this qualitatively different from what we do on a national or international scale? As Michael Foucault notes, "War is politics pursued by other means; politics is war pursued by other means." In such cases, goodness is the first and last casualty.[1]

In order to keep tragedy from happening, we must refuse to take sides, which requires a tremendous amount of courage. A person seeking to do it will be perceived as a traitor by friends and a fool by enemies. No more fearful territory exists than the no man's land among hostile extremes. Yet, that's where God requires us to stand if we are to share in his goodness,

---

1. Foucault, *Society Defended*, 15.

resisting the urgings and temptations of friends and foes alike. Alone there, we can discover whether or not our heart is fixed, trusting in the Lord. What does God promise us if we can stand in that place, that nexus of love and courage: a gift of goodness not requiring us to spend our vital energy nursing grudges or engineering machinations that perish when we no longer live.

Psalm 113

"He raiseth up the poor out of the dust, and lifteth the needy out of the dunghill." (Ps 113:7)

Never is charity more at risk than when people pride themselves on being charitable. Never are people less spiritual than when they insist on being religious. Never is God more divine than when he shares our humanity.

In our ill-fated attempts to become gods, we forget that God humbled himself to become one of us. According to the Psalmist, it is God's nature to be humble and to raise up those who are humiliated by the world's princes: "he raiseth up the poor out of the dust, and lifteth the needy out of the dunghill." Is it any wonder Jesus says, "Blessed are the poor for theirs is the kingdom of heaven"? To share in a poverty of spirit is to be the recipient of God's wealth.

There are mornings I leave home with the weight of despair on my shoulders at all the abuses and misuses of power by those in charge—mandarins who see the world as their oyster. Their ways are all too predictable.

Not so with God. His ways are ever new. Just this morning I noticed that winter had turned. Light seeps into the sky earlier now. The horizon was streaked with lavender even as a single star still blinked in the west. The whole panorama took my breath, and I understood the pang of gratitude the Psalmist felt in declaring, "From the rising of the sun into the going down of the same the Lord's name is to be praised."

It is not enough for us to want to be like gods. We must want to be like God. And that means imitating his humility, emptying ourselves of all our vain claims to power, dying to all but the desire to be part of a creation that is already perfect.

Psalm 114

"Tremble, thou earth, at the presence of the Lord, at the presence of the God of Jacob." (PS114:7)

The Psalmist is almost giddy at the way nature and man quake before God. In some of the most whimsical and delightful imagery found in the Bible, he recalls how "the mountains skipped like rams, and the little hills like lambs" in the presence of the Lord. The message is clear: What enemy can withstand such a God?

What this situation underscores is that our Bible is a lengthy account of battles, or wars, and captains of wars. James Hillman notes that "Yahweh presents himself in the speeches of a War God, and his prophets and kinds are his warriors. Even the New Testament is so arranged that its final culminating chapter, Revelation, functions as its recapitulative coda in which the Great Armageddon of the Apocalypse is its crisis."[1]

Hillman also points out an elemental fact of human nature that few people want to recognize: Wars do not arise simply from "industrial capitalism and its economic distress, the mystiques of tribes and nationalism, the just preservation of a state, masculine machismo, sociological indoctrinations or psychological paranoia and aggression."[2] Rather, war bears witness to something essentially human that transcends the human, something almost impossible for humans to grasp. Only mythology serves us in providing an explanation and in invoking the divine spirit of war in such personifications as Mars. Merely denying the impulse to make war is counterproductive. We must internalize the desire and transform it, taking the battle to the place where it actually exists: within us. As Sufi master Bawa Muhaiyadden observes, true jihad is not taking others' lives: "True jihad is

---

1. Hillman, *Essential*, 181.
2. Hillman, *Essential*, 182.

to praise God and cut away the inner satanic enemies."[3] Jesus too emphasizes the true nature of this warfare, saying, "And fear not them which kill the body, but are not able to kill the soul: but rather fear him which is able to kill both body and soul in hell."

Every day I pray for the archangels to protect my extended family and me and to extend that protection throughout the world. I also pray the "Our Father," or "Lord's Prayer," lingering over the line: "Lead us not into temptation but deliver us from evil." As with most things Jesus says, this utterance offers a double-edged sword. On the one hand, it is a plea to protect us from all the evil, the harm, people can do to us, both physically and spiritually. On the other hand, it can constitute an appeal to protect others from the evil of our own actions. Because so much of human motivation is shrouded in the darkness of the unconscious and because we are too often blind to our own intentions, we need God's help in protecting us from ourselves. In praying Jesus's prayer, we are calling upon the warrior spirit of God to embolden us with love, awareness, gentleness, and courage. These are qualities that turn "flint into a fountain of waters."

---

3. Muhaiyadden, "Holy War."

Psalm 115

"The dead praise not the Lord, neither any that go down into silence."
(Ps 115:17)

The Psalmist is simply reminding us that life here on earth is the time for praising the Lord. Life itself is a gift deserving of praise. As a middle-aged orphan whose parents have been dead for many years, I'm aware that I have no buffers between me and my mortality. There comes a point in life where you've known as many dead people as you know living ones. Their voices haunt you in memory, and you find yourself talking to them, wishing for the opportunity not to have to invent their reply. Sometimes they speak most clearly in dreams, revealing items about themselves you thought you'd forgotten. But the biggest, most pleasant surprise is when I hear echoes of their presence in my own voice. That's when I know they're still very much alive in ways that approach the profoundest mystery. Just yesterday I heard my father's poetry in something I said to my son. My son was going to a local bookstore when I had the sudden impulse to give him twenty dollars for which he has not asked. "Just a little something to sweeten the pot," I said, recalling the phrase my father used whenever he wanted to make sure I had more than I needed just to get by. Like the boy I was then, my son thanked me, expressing gratitude for a gift offered to us both.

Psalm 116

"The sorrows of death compassed me, and the pains of hell gat hold upon me: I found trouble and sorrow." (Ps 116:3)

At times in my life when fear has overtaken me, I have recited this psalm as a comforting mantra. It begins in the depths of distress: "The sorrows of death compassed me, and the pains of hell compassed on me." This situation prompts the Psalmist to call upon the Lord, almost as an afterthought. The rest of the poem expresses gratitude to the God who takes the sentence of death and despair upon himself, freeing us of these burdens and enabling us to "walk in the land of the living." As a result, the Psalmist gains a crucial insight: By walking in death before us, God shows us the way to life. How else to explain the divine alchemy by which unutterable death is transformed into a triumphant declaration: "Precious in the sight of the Lord is the death of his saints"? This isn't resignation; this is jubilation, based on the assurance that anywhere the Lord remains is preferable to anywhere he isn't—even if that place is the cross. Chronologically speaking, death is the last thing we ever have to fear. Without the fear of death, all other anxieties dissolve, and we are free to live in the peace of souls at rest. How much better to live without that fear before the time of our dying. The Psalmist offers a kernel of this spiritual logic when he says, "Return unto thy rest, O my soul; for the Lord hath dealt bountifully with thee."

Psalm 117

"O praise the LORD, all ye nations: praise him, all ye people." (Ps 117:1)

Only thirty-three words long, this psalm restores a proper balance to the world by giving it back to God, its creator. What a far cry from the fantasies of "globalism" and global markets we perpetuate in our time. Woe be unto those few refusing to embrace the collective stereotypes that we're told are our only choices if we are to be part of this world. Not to be "connected" is to be nothing or to have one's genuine identity nullified. We must constantly be doing: internet chatting, mobile phoning, twenty-four-hour texting, and frantically planning if we're to have a stake in a future as perilous and anxiety-ridden as the present.

Fortunately, God offers an alternative to a commercial hell characterized by the fearful dimensions of human proximity and separation. We do not have to belong to a world the mass market fanaticists claim they own. Nor are we required to worship their idols, which demand sacrifices of inestimable time and energy while promising freedom that never materializes.

What we have to do is claim our autonomy as children of the living God, being reborn if necessary and rejecting the death around us. Being reborn has nothing to do with rituals of fundamentalism and the misunderstanding surrounding them. Those rituals can be just as suffocating and death-inducing as the culture that sanctions them. Instead, we must reject the many disguises of death, which often pose as commodities we can't afford to live without. After all, few are satisfied with what they have and even fewer can decide what they want.

Only God who made us, the God of "all nations," knows our needs because only he can plumb the mystery of our being. Being one with us, he knows us in ways concealed from those who have only one way of seeing a thing and whose limitations are all too humanly apparent if we just stop to notice.

Psalm 118

"The Lord is on my side; I will not fear: what can man do unto me?"
(Ps 118:6)

Wendell Berry writes that "the older love becomes, the more clearly it understands its involvement in partiality, imperfection, suffering, and mortality. Even so, it longs for incarnation."[1] This psalm contains two of the humblest attestations of faith imaginable: "The Lord is on my side" and "The Lord takes my part." The certainty here is absolute.

All my life I've heard the phrase "take his (or her) part" in describing how parents will go to any lengths to defend their children even when those children are in the wrong. It's not that parents are necessarily impervious to the wrongdoings of their children. The parents may be terribly ambivalent, desirous of punishing the children themselves. The ferocious, irrational nature of love overrides any and all threats to the child. It's a rare parent who wouldn't beg, lie, cheat, and steal to keep a child from experiencing serious repercussions from some crime the child has committed.

I remember my own parents taking my part at times when I didn't deserve their interventions. They protected me from the outrageous consequences of my own actions. No doubt they felt ashamed of me at times when I placed them in the position of compromising their own principles. In every case, however, this is what love does: it suspends judgment, being or breaking the law on our behalf. If this were not so, love would be the exclusive possession of a small number of perfect *saints*.

Fortunately, God sees us for who we are and loves us anyway. In his perfection, he takes the part of his imperfect children, defending us against our own worst impulses and often against the righteous judgments of others. Because he is partial to us as individuals, he loves us not as abstractions,

---

1. Berry, "Word and Flesh," 200.

Psalm 118

but as children, each of whom has a history and a relationship with him that belongs to no other. His love breaks every rule on our behalf. There isn't one of us for whom he won't forsake his own judgments and principles, humbly bearing the shame we cause him while taking our part.

Psalm 119

"Deal bountifully with thy servant that I may live, and keep thy word."
(Ps 119:17)

This psalm is an oratorio, each voice expressing the "groaning" that St. Paul says issues from our souls. This groaning is a result of our soul's need to be united with God eternally. On the one hand, we struggle toward God. On the other hand, we fear answering the call that leads to total inner transformation. We are attracted and repulsed simultaneously. Like children suddenly aware that they are swimming in water over their heads, we are paralyzed with terror.

Marion Woodman asks, "Why are we so afraid to change? Why, when we are so desperate for change, do we become even more desperate when transformation begins? Why do we lose our childhood's faith in growing? Why do we cling to old attachments instead of submitting ourselves to new possibilities—to the undiscovered worlds in our own bodies, minds, and souls?"[1]

The obvious answer is that we cannot endure what seems to be an intolerable contradiction: Birth is the death of the life we have known; death is the birth of the life we have yet to live. Life is full of many little deaths and even some big ones. Conditioned by so much death in life, we freeze at the gargantuan task of seeking life in death. Nor do we have the luxury of naiveté we had when we were younger.

At present, our youngest son, the last of the children to leave home, is pulling out of the driveway, ready to make his morning commute to the local college, part of a larger adventure from which his mother and I will eventually be cut off. Even if he remains home a couple of years more, we are aware of the psychic distance necessary for him to strike out and find

---

1. Woodman, "Interview," 64–75.

his own path. We will always represent home for him. But home will never be the same for us. My wife offers the stark reminder: "We've been rearing children all our adult lives." The question is: what next?

We're at a crossroads, finding ourselves at the heart of a new mystery. I can't help but grieve at losing something for which I don't yet see the possibility of transformation. At such a pass, I confess that my tendency is to resurrect old habits of avoidance and to indulge familiar compulsions. In a state of anxiety, even destructive habits can be viewed as friends providing much needed comfort.

All that only postpones the inevitable. Besides, who would forsake the path after spending so much time pursuing it? Maybe that's why the voices in this psalm are almost fanatical in asking God not to let them "wander" from the Way, getting sidetracked by following the many death-in-life options promising temporary comfort. The problem is that they are only temporary. Indulging them for too long causes its own problems.

I'm reminded of a poem by Robert Frost in which the speaker stops by woods on a snowy evening for reasons not entirely known to him. It is "the darkest evening of the year" so that even the speaker's horse "gives his harness bells a shake / To ask if there is some mistake." But the speaker remains, lost in the hypnotic radiance of a scene whose attraction is *thanatos*, the death wish.[2]

How tempting it is at this point in my life to succumb to the sleep that marks despair, including the alternative to rest on my laurels. I could lapse into regression or wait for someone else to do something. Plenty of people enlist the aid of the unconscious, sinking into chronic illness or embracing rigidity and psychic death. Lord protect me from the unconscious manifestations of my desire to remain in stasis, what spiritual journeymen once termed *acedia*.

What I know is that death and rebirth can be excruciating transitions. And it is sometimes hard to see the hand of love in these cyclic operations. What is required is a leap of faith I steadfastly refuse to make for fear of annihilating all that is beloved and familiar to me. Just knowing this fact is an indication of divine grace stirring within me. The next step may simply be to repeat the words that the Psalmist, out of the depths of despair, finds rising to his lips: "Let thy tender mercies come to me that I may live."

---

2. Frost, "Stopping by Woods," 9–10.

Psalm 120

"My soul hath dwelt with him that hath peace. I am for peace: but when I speak, they are for war." (Ps 120:6–7)

Jesus could not extricate himself from the politics of his day. Nor can we, unfortunately. Genuine spiritual initiatives always find themselves at odds with power structures imbued with consumerism, ambition, and narcissistic fantasies.

Even now, the reasons our government gave for initiating a war with Iraq are not the reasons used to justify continuing that war. Last year at my college, I gave a presentation to several hundred people showing how the pre-emptive war we were waging didn't fulfill a single criterion of the Just War Doctrine, the test by which Christians have traditionally decided whether to use violence or not. This teaching owes its existence to St. Augustine and its more refined status to St. Thomas Aquinas, both declaring war an evil and violence a last resort. Neither of these was a consideration in attacking Iraq.

To say that my position was unpopular at the time is an understatement of cosmic proportions. To counter my avowed opposition, the local National Guard brought its NASCAR racing automobile to campus as a recruiting tool. After my speech, dozens of students e-mailed and later visited the college's administration, demanding that I be "punished" or fired. One local state senator mentioned trying me for treason under the War Powers Act.

All of that was before hundreds of Americans and untold numbers of Iraqis were killed and before the motives for going to war began to be scrutinized in the public domain. The administration in Washington tried to say it wasn't to blame for the mess because its intelligence was "faulty." In hospitals in Baghdad, children lay without limbs or sight. Profiteers continued to secure funds for the "clean-up" effort.

What I know is that good Christians everywhere supported this war and hated those of us who opposed it. The rancor shown us was venomous. Later those same people began to complain about the failures of the war. I suppose there's some consolation in being able to say better late than never. Frankly, that's just too disgusting an option for me to consider. People are responsible for their own consciences, not having to depend on others to do the right thing for them.

National self-righteousness is as sinful as the personal kind, and waging war just because we can or because it serves our economic interests is so horrifyingly banal as to register no jitter on the moral compass. What occurs to me is that I don't want anyone's children maimed or killed for my benefit. Not one. If that means weathering storms of protest until the rhetoric subsides and the war-paint fades, then I'll wait for Him who calmed the waves and promised not to leave me comfortless.

Psalm 121

"I will lift up mine eyes unto the hills, from whence cometh my help."
(Ps 121:1)

In the words of Parker J. Palmer, "Fear is fundamental to the human condition. We will always have our fear—but we need not be our fears." He further claims that "spirituality and the religious traditions are, at bottom, about living in the face of fear."[1] I'm inclined to agree. The plainest cruelties and needs of human existence drive us to be afraid and to commit violence with all the justification fear affords. Fear can make us do anything—literally.

Palmer's distinction is especially helpful to me as a college teacher. I'm not afraid of my students. But more and more I am afraid of what they're becoming. In one of my classes yesterday, I showed a brilliant documentary by film maker Ross Spears. *To Render a Life* is a portrait of a contemporary, poor rural family living under conditions strikingly similar to those faced by Depression-era sharecroppers. Living on the brink of survival in one of the richest counties in America in the 1990s, the Glass family received no government or social welfare assistance. They had no health insurance and weren't eligible for Medicare. Despite having worked 31 years finishing furniture for a local firm, the family's father could not collect Social Security benefits, nor was he enrolled in a retirement program. The family's mother, aged 48 at the time of the filming, had suffered a stroke that worsened an existing heart condition. To top it all, the couple was trying to rear their eight-year-old granddaughter with deafness.[2]

I wondered whether learning to see what James Agee described as the "sorrowful holiness" of such people wasn't essential to the education of our

---

1. Palmer, *Courage*, 58.
2. Spears, *Render Life*, Agee Films.

hearts.[3] The resistance was immediate. Apparently, a characteristic of the new culture of disconnection is to be numb to the suffering of others and to have contempt for anyone who reminds us that, in a very real sense, we are our brother's keeper.

Not so, argued a disturbing majority of the class. In almost all cases, they said, the poor being lazy and shiftless are to blame not only for their own plight, but for the moral confusion they cause the rest of us. The anger threatened to overflow like a volcano.

"Well," I said, "Jesus doesn't make a distinction between the deserving and undeserving poor; does he?"

I was taking a chance that some genuine vestige of the Christianity they all claim to profess might strike a chord of compassion.

"What does that have to do with it?" one young man asked, his lip curling in a snarl.

Obviously nothing, I thought. Still, I reminded them that a tradition of Christian charity undergirds many of the activities of social agencies and even the policies of government designed to help people who are treated unjustly and on whom doors are constantly slammed because there is no room at the inn.

"There's too much government as it is," railed another young man, repeating the tirade he'd probably heard on the radio on his way to class. "The churches ought to do more so that the government won't have to do it. It's the churches' responsibility to help people."

"I agree," I pointed out. "But using your own argument, if we wait for the churches to step up and do what they should to help the poor, then we'll be waiting till hell freezes over."

He'd set a trap for himself and walked into it. Almost all of them had. Their surly silence said it all. It wasn't an issue of who would help those victimized by cruel poverty; it was an effort at figuring out how not to help at all.

Having just seen a film exploding every stereotype about the undeserving poor, my students chose not to invoke enough imagination to consider that, but for the Grace of God and the ferocious hand of fate, there go every one of us. Who withstands the furious assaults of the universe? How we treat the poor in all their many guises, Jesus points out, is a judgment upon ourselves. That means not letting our fears calcify into hard-heartedness,

---

3. Agee, *Famous Men*, 134.

giving us a way to avoid looking at the wounds of the single, unrepeatable, and holy individuals around us.

Psalm 122

"Peace be within thee." (Ps 122:8)

It goes without saying that the peace can be disturbed. Human beings with their free will can choose discord. As I tell my creative writing students, if you want to create conflict in a story, throw in two characters, each with different goals. Automatically, sparks will fly and poison will seep into the plot.

Violence is such a commonplace ritual in our society that periods of peace make us uncomfortable. People who, under ordinary circumstances, would deny believing in evolution see nothing wrong with draconian, dog-eat-dog practices inspired by our economic system. In such a system, charity is seen as a contemptible weakness because common wisdom has it that people ought to be able to pull themselves up by their bootstraps. If they can't, they don't deserve life's fruits.

That means pushing people out of the way when necessary. It's nothing personal, of course, just part of the routine tasks and daily unpleasantness, a systematic program of violence we take for granted. Only a fool would refuse to participate—literally.

Interesting figure—the Fool. They exist in almost every culture as a counterpoint to bloated egos so full of self-will and self-interests as to hear no voices but their own. By contrast, fools are empty of all desires; and because they have no desires, they don't find themselves in conflict. They don't rush or rant.

According to the French monk and writer Francois Rabelais, "the fool is a perfect Christian, since he cares nothing for earthly wealth and fame. One must be unmindful of self in order to appear wise enough before the celestial intelligences to receive the gift of divination. Everything which appears important here on earth must be set aside in a quiescent state which is commonly imputed to madness."[1]

According to these criteria, Jesus and his disciples were perfect fools, just as they were often regarded by the vulgar crowds heckling them. Consider: "therefore I say unto you, Take no thought for your life, what ye shall eat, or what ye shall drink; nor yet for your body, what ye shall put on. Is life not more than meat, and the body than raiment?" Only a fool would say such a thing. Only someone emptied of all desires but the desire to surrender one's will, living in at-one-ment with God, could be so insane as to assert: "But I say unto you, Love your enemies, bless them that curse you, do good to them that hate you, and pray for them which despitefully use you, and persecute you." Such a declaration flies in the face of conventional wisdom. What reasonable person would accept this injunction? The answer is that no merely reasonable person would.

What I'm beginning to understand is that anyone not subscribing to the laws, or lawlessness, of the jungle is going to be viewed as a fool by the "wise" people of the world. The wise know what they want and how to get it. They are full of answers, inspiring envy and admiration. They navigate the world with ease.

Fools are never at home in the world. They are awkward, out of place, left behind. When people say, "Only a fool would love his enemies," the fools believe them, giving up their own desires and doing the unthinkable. Fools know no limits to forgiveness. Countless times they are buffeted and tormented but go back for more. Their madness, cloaked in motley, disguises their royal lineage as princes of peace. Born out of our deepest desires for affection and acceptance, they are the children of God who love us to our great and everlasting embarrassment.

---

1. Rabelais, *Third Book*.

Psalm 123

"Have mercy upon us." (Ps 123:3)

The way is perilous, nor is there one of us who doesn't feel the enormous assaults of the universe as we reside here locked between the stale earth and the sky. At every moment, if we are sentient, we are aware of straddling the deepest divide of pity, terror, doubt, and guilt. How better to describe the human soul than as a furious angel nailed to the ground by its wings? And who could ever anticipate the fate of such a creature over the long haul of its living, breathing existence? To be born into time is to participate in a sad waltz, a requiem for ourselves and those other mysterious presences we encounter.

Who knows why we are placed in living proximity to those who, by another name, we choose to call friends? All I know is that long ago I shared the period of childhood with such a one as James who, by a series of merciful linguistic transformations, became Jimbo, then Bo, to all who knew him. As a boy, he had a good and charitable heart and sunshine for a face. Although seeing him little after college, I was told he carried those same qualities into adulthood. But my memories are of a much earlier time—when a single day stretched out in endless possibilities, and play was the serious, unending business of our young lives. What an impression we must have made on the nearby woods with our paths and treehouses and forts built low to the ground. Once we dug a hole big enough to bury someone. Tiring of that, we scavenged coke bottles for the deposits they'd bring. Bo's dog had three legs but would follow us anyway. There was something unnamable in what we were doing and something I've never been able to capture since. About the only times I saw Bo after that were those occasions when someone in the old neighborhood died, and we assembled for a funeral. Such was the case a year or so ago when we gathered to pay our respects to the mother of a mutual friend.

On spotting Bo, I saw him grin, his eyes etched in lines from a lifetime of flashing that self-same smile. He was heavy, the way his father had been, but still carried himself like the athlete of his youth. All manner of memories flooded my consciousness, and I suddenly recalled how he'd been a collector of things: rocks, bugs, baseball cards, and it didn't really matter. Within inches of embracing each other, he held up a hand: "I've got the crud, and I don't want to give it to you." Turning to his brother, he said "Hug him for me, Davie." Davie did the honors. We laughed.

Months passed. I received the call while on a boat in the North Sea. Bo had shot and killed himself after interminable agony from chronic back ailment. The painkillers apparently hadn't worked, and his job required him to perform constant lifting. His wife, returning from a trip to the supermarket, had found him. On the pillow next to his head lay a gun—one of hundreds he'd collected over the years. Ironically, no one could remember his ever having fired any of them.

Being thousands of miles away, I was unable to make the funeral. I do know that the Catholic Church considers suicide a sin deserving hell. Such a belief indicates the way people without imaginations are inclined to think. How fortunate for us such considerations are ultimately in the hands of God.

One thing I can say for certain is that my friend, not wanting me to catch what he was carrying the last time I saw him, must have been in unimaginable pain for him to kill himself. I can only surmise that everything in his life had brought him to that point. The mystery of it all is overwhelming. For that reason, I'll suspend any judgment and resist any effort to explain what can't be known. Better to recall one merciful day in summer when a boy with a made-up name set out on an undisclosed path, collecting things along the way.

Psalm 124

"If it had not been the Lord who was on our side . . ." (Ps 124:1)

Today my wife Linda and I are celebrating our twenty-fifth wedding anniversary. It had to have been God's grace that we came together. Nothing else explains it. In the beginning there were times we were as petulant as children, each of us struggling to hold on to some sense of self we thought we couldn't live without. The politics of marriage can be brutal at times, especially when the partners are jockeying for power, dominance, and identity. Yoked together, married people often pull in opposite directions. It's a wonder any marriage withstands the tension.

Under no circumstances am I offering advice for achieving a successful marriage. I have no ideas what that means. I do, however, suspect God was on our side on many occasions when we didn't know it. For my part, my marriage to Linda has been an education of the heart so that I no longer know where I end and she begins. Sometimes at night I awaken, staying up just to listen to her breathe. My heart races, and my mind offers a desperate prayer that she stays safe and we continue our life together for years to come. And what are years but days like the ones we've spent becoming the people we could never have been without each other? What could be more precious than being able to rub lotion on her back or to hear the music in her voice on the phone when I call for no particular reason?

Before we married, I sat down one day on a moving crate and wrote a poem, an epithalamion, or marriage hymn, for her. I confess it was practically an afterthought though I should have approached such an undertaking with fear and trembling. Fortunately, youth protected me from the consequences of my naiveté. How could I have known that what I wrote would grow truer and deeper than I could ever have imagined or that she and I would share a soul's journey that would blossom into a paradox, finding us wanting more the less time we have? Sometimes my heart aches when I realize that so much of it is behind us, but then I stand in awe of the distance we've traveled together on a path marked by births and deaths of all sorts and the grace of the horizon still before us.

On that February day 25 years ago, I had no idea to what extent I'd never be the same. I knew I loved this woman, this single unrepeatable being, who mysteriously drew me to her, body and soul. What I couldn't see was the silent unnamable presence accompanying us, embracing us in our embraces, and refusing to let us go.

Psalm 125

"For the rod of the wicked shall not rest upon the lot of the righteous."
(Ps 125:3)

I'm always amazed at the process of selective literalism, the method of choosing Bible verses, by which people justify condemning others. Pick and choose—there's no end to the mischief people can do.

Take the recent condemnation of homosexuals by many of the leading lights found in our video pulpits today. One is inclined to ask why they target gays to the exclusion of all the other "sinners" they could sight down in their crosshairs. Imagine my students' surprise on discovering during one recent class that plenty of transgressions are routinely ignored by the current tribe of electronic Pharisees. I was referring specifically to those passages in Leviticus where homosexuality is only one of a multitude of "abominations" deserving of severe punishment and even death. Interesting to note is that when a person sins in the Old Testament, he's supposed to bring a "trespass offering" of one ram to be slaughtered by the priest. I don't see many evangelicals requiring that today, I pointed out. Maybe they're a bit lax in their standards.

There are other signs that they may be emphasizing some crimes to the exclusion of others. For instance, among the ancient Hebrews talking back to one's parents could obtain the death penalty for a child. Not many of us would have survived that test.

Psalm 126

"They that sow in tears shall reap in joy." (Ps 126:5)

William Carlos Williams has a poem in which the speaker, a woman, begins by saying, "Sorrow is my own yard." Recently widowed, the woman can't bear the approach of spring with its promise of renewal. Her heart is full of unspeakable anguish so that she confesses to wanting to drown herself in a nearby marsh strewn with white flowers.[1]

A year or so ago, my uncle died, leaving my aunt in a similar predicament. They'd lived together for 55 years, often joking how they were joined at the hip. It's hard to imagine a couple who enjoyed each other more. They were partners in every way.

Above all, my uncle was a gentleman. I read once that a gentleman is someone who does what needs doing, then stays out of the way the rest of the time. That described my Uncle Bob. He was a solid, steadying influence. His love blossomed in silence. My Aunt Mona, on the other hand, tended to be more emotional and expressive. She was his music in all its many moods.

I worried that his death would cause her spirit to wither. The pain of separation she experienced was physical—like an addict enduring withdrawal. Nevertheless, she refused her doctor's prescriptions for sedatives and anti-depressants. She wanted to feel everything associated with her beloved husband, even the anguish of his absence. She didn't want to be numb to any of it. I admired her for that.

Following his death, she had his body cremated, and in a special ceremony with only a few family in attendance, she spread his ashes next to a stream on the edge of their property. That way, she could sit on the deck, she said, and watch him give birth to the livery of flowers and shrubs they'd

---

1. Williams, "Widow's Lament," 1.

PSALM 126

planted together over the years. She hoped the bitter winter would end soon.

That was more than a year ago, and she is feeling better now. Her voice is stronger. Many times the grace of healing occurs without our full awareness. She has settled my uncle's estate, reads late into the night, and sometimes walks about the house. Once she dreamed he was lying next to her in bed. When she awoke, she said she could smell him.

The awful gulf between them does not seem as wide as it did when he first passed away. And her time here is more tolerable, even hopeful, knowing that all the tears will reap untold joys when their living spirits are reunited. Just the other day she told me on the phone how much she was looking forward to spring.

Psalm 127

"Except the Lord build the house, they labor in vain that build it."
(Ps 127:1)

The Franciscan priest Richard Rohr writes, "Even though we can't see God, we can discover God in what God has created."[1] One (and only one) of God's creations happens to be us. As Genesis tells/reveals to us: "God created humankind in God's own imagine; male and female God created them." This verse would seem to settle the issue about whether God is masculine or feminine. Clearly God is neither one exclusively, but both simultaneously.

Yet the Psalmist needs a warrior God, one who can dominate the enemies of Israel, so he naturally projects onto God a masculine image. Extending this trope, he compares children to "arrows in the hands of a mighty man," an unfortunate choice of language by one firmly rooted in the context of the times.

The saner and more spiritually accurate view of children finds them as divine creations close to the heart of a loving God. No less than Jesus himself reminds us that God would gladly be a hen and take us under his wings like little chicks. Further, Jesus warns a conniving and indifferent world not to neglect "the least of these"[2] or to do anything that would otherwise separate God from his children since "of such is the kingdom of Heaven."[3] Only by becoming as little children, trusting and loving God wholeheartedly, can we experience God as other than a fearful projection of nightmarish proportions.

1. Rohr, "Creation and Incarnation."
2. Matt 25:40.
3. Matt 19:14.

Psalm 127

I refuse to accept a God like that. My God is not a sadist, and I do not have to bow and scrape in his presence. Just like Jesus, I can call him "Abba" or Daddy. Some people might argue that I'm on dangerous ground here, that God requires sycophants and servants willing to obey rules blindly. That ignores the fact that Jesus corrected such a vision of God, calling upon us not to injure one another just as God would never injure us. And as God would give his life for us, so are we to give our lives for one another. To live peaceably in the kingdom of the divine heart and to love naturally as we were created to do—these are the only conditions God asks of us.

Psalm 128

"The LORD shall bless thee out of Zion: and thou shalt see the good of Jerusalem all the days of thy life." (Ps 128:5)

I'm 51 today. I awoke in awe (and maybe even a little terror) this morning, realizing that everything in my life has led me to this moment. Everything, even the pain and disappointments, have been sacred. I place it all before the throne of God.

Wordsworth says that "the Child is father of the Man."[1] Who of us can begin to account for the mysterious circumstances of our origins? Why was I placed in the care of the people who reared me? And what does that period of my life, a time of spiritual and psychological formation, have to do with me now? It hardly matters that they were imperfect people, lacking in ways of us all, pelted by the universe from countless directions, and manifesting the by-products of our original condition passed from generation to generation. I can't help but forgive them, for their failures are ones that belong to us all. Saying I forgive them is another way of acknowledging that there's nothing to forgive. At the deepest level of our humanity, my parents were gifts to me, giving me an unspeakably mysterious existence. What difference does it make that the day I chose to enter this life was a cold one? Or that all of us get bogged down with the sad effects of the second law of thermodynamics? Isn't it sadness that gives a song its beauty? Life, my life, is sacred just as it is. God-given, it needs no excuse or justification.

I just poured my son a cup of coffee and roused him from sleep so he can attend classes at the university. My wife is out of town, but she wants my son and me to have dinner this evening at a nice restaurant. It will not be an ordinary event (there are no such things) because life is charged with a mystery embracing all the presences—living and dead—we've ever

---

1. Wordsworth, "My Heart," 7.

encountered. They'll all be seated around us at the sacramental table where everyone has a place, and no one is denied. It will be all I can do to keep from shouting with joy.

Psalm 129

"Many a time have they afflicted me from my youth . . . yet they have not prevailed against me." (Ps 129:1, 2b)

Anger, disappointment, fear, and uncertainty—the four horsemen of my private apocalypse. Imagine if I were able to bless these companions and send them on their way. What expansive freedom I would experience in the chambers of my heart! How I'd have no need to fix everything and everyone around me! In other words, I'd feel no desire to *convert* anyone.

Pema Chodron, the Buddhist nun, says that "The view of the spiritual warrior is not 'Hell is bad and heaven is good' or 'Get rid of hell and just seek heaven.' Instead, we encourage ourselves to develop an open heart and an open mind to heaven, to heal, to everything. Only with this kind of equanimity can we realize that no matter what comes along, we're always standing in the middle of a sacred place!"[1]

I seem to be at a crossroads now, a physical and psychic junction tending to inspire pity and terror. At 51, I don't let a day pass without tallying my failures or trying to justify my life in terms of my so-called successes. Both of these activities are ingrained habits. Both miss the point that I have an opportunity to stand in a new place of freedom and to develop the practices of the spiritual warrior whom we all have a chance to be. For some time now, I've been avoiding facing this opportunity, preferring the moribund option of numbing myself to the pain and heartache of leaving my old life behind rather than it, me and all I've learned, good or bad, into a new arena of struggle. For too long now, I've been drinking too much, working too hard, and trying to be all things to all people. These futile struggles have kept me from a full realization that the kingdom is at hand.

---

1. Chodron, *Awakening*, 61–62.

Psalm 129

Today I'm going to try to remain open, to experience and not to classify. I'm going to try to muster the courage to feel what I'm feeling and see where those sensations lead me. Most of all, I want to give myself permission to acknowledge the four companions of my youth while letting their influences diminish over time. To make this effort conscious rather than sliding back into unconsciousness is no easy task. It will require giving up what I've grown all my life to believe I can't live without and accepting what only grace can convince me I truly need. That means dying to old habits that no longer satisfy the requirements of developing my soul in the time allotted me and instead embracing possibilities of new life my faith tells me are unimaginable.

Psalm 130

"My soul waiteth for the Lord more than they that watch for morning."
(Ps 130:6)

I stopped in my tracks this morning, glancing out the window, struck by the spectacle of the most beautiful sky I'd ever seen. For a moment it mesmerized me. Like colors bleeding on a canvas, crimsons and oranges streaked an intense blue canopy, and for a while I took delight in knowing that no human hand had a part in creating so splendid a thing. It was a comfort to my soul.

   Later, I went upstairs to wake my son; and there, to my surprise and delight, his face was bathed in the same hues, as if the source of that light was reaching beyond itself, finding entrance at the window, and coming to rest on one of the persons most precious to me. It was hard to tell where the divine light began and the human reflection ended, though as for that, it didn't seem to matter. It was all the same. I couldn't imagine a better blessing or a finer memory to recall when the sky is slate-gray and the light is slow in breaking.

Psalm 131

"Lord, my heart is not haughty, nor mine eyes lofty: neither do I exercise myself in great matters or in things too high for me." (Ps 131:1)

It's all too common though it never ceases to shock. A baby-faced, sixteen-year-old boy here had a dispute with his mother. She went next door and called the police. A single officer responded to the call, exiting the car in the crosshairs of an assault rifle. The officer never knew what hit him. The twenty-four-year-old policeman's wife was expecting a baby any day.

One can only imagine the panic and despair that the boy, locked behind the walls of his house, was experiencing. He exchanged a few more shots with the more than one hundred officers and several SWAT teams who immediately arrived on the scene. Outside friends and neighbors registered the appropriate levels of shock. School chums described their barricaded friend as a normal, funny kid who'd nonetheless slashed his wrists a while back, prompting a period of psychiatric hospitalization.

Some of the neighbors expressed disbelief that such a "Columbine-like" circumstance could occur in their own upscale neighborhood. The father was, incidentally, an assistant district attorney general for the county. In the newspaper, the parents were described as "caring and compassionate." I do not doubt it.

The only blip on the screen, besides the obvious emotional upheaval the boy had earlier experienced was what police described as an "arsenal" of high-powered weapons in the house, including semi-automatic assault rifles. But as people here are fond of saying, "Guns don't kill people; people kill people." What that tidy truism fails to account for is that guns are designed for one purpose only. Merely wounding someone is perceived as a failure.

So we are left with a mystery of sorts, though I don't know if it's as mysterious as all that. There's something comforting, I suppose, in one local minister's assessment that "the boy just snapped. If you had tried to make sense of it, you'd go nuts." What I know is that every parent honest with him-or-herself, shivered a bit, glad for the opportunity to say, "But for the grace of God" —whatever that means in such a situation.

No, I'm not ready to give up on finding out what all too often happens to our young people though I have no desire to blame anyone either, too many suffering forces to engage in dark whispering and silent finger pointing. Let all fingers point inward into the sacrosanct characters of our wounded hearts.

Still, even before the boy's immediate fate was decided, people were putting him on trial, advancing the possibility of the death penalty despite his status as a minor. He saved them the trouble, shooting himself in the head in the upstairs bedroom. What loneliness and child's terror he must have experienced in that interminable eternity before pulling the trigger! Who can say it wasn't a final act of penance for a mistake he wholeheartedly regretted? As a father, I can only subscribe to that possibility. As a father, I can only grieve that a baby, soon to be born, will grow up fatherless, deprived of the smiling affection of one who answered a call without sufficient knowledge of what might happen.

Who knows by what mysterious circumstances our destinies are intertwined? Perhaps no occurrences are accidental, especially if the law of life really is sacrifice: giving our lives for one another. I pray that God takes both these young men into his timeless care, clothes them, and sets them down to a banquet in each other's presence where they will get to know one another as they were meant. I hope the same for the rest of us whose woundedness is all too apparent to anyone willing to see.

Psalm 132

"Let thy priests be clothed with righteousness; and let thy saints shout for joy." (Ps 132:9)

I've put off writing this meditation. My church and many of its priests are currently involved in scandal, and I, along with many other people, feel wounded and distrustful, knowing that we may never have the same relationship with the church we once had. That is not to say I have written off the church and its clergy *carte blanche*. It's just that I'm being watchful, redefining my notion of "the priesthood of believers" in a more expansive way. I no longer believe that just because a person wears a collar, he is a priest. Being a priest is an attitude, in the old religious sense of the term. A priest can no more save my soul than he can save his own. Indeed, unless today's priest is committed to a renewed sense of self and to the avoidance of groupthink, including the church's variety, he serves little purpose. No one can be a spokesperson for the party line and be a real priest.

Perhaps it's always been so. A week ago in a used bookstore, I bought a ten-cent copy of Martin Luther King, Jr.'s *Strength to Love*, a book of Dr. King's sermons published shortly after his death. They're absolutely remarkable. Even the titles of the sermons suggest a man engaged in all of life's perplexities, demonstrating an existential courage too often lacking in our own time: "Transformed Nonconformist," "Loving Your Enemies," "The Man Who Was a Fool," and "Antidotes to Bear." Of course, most school children are familiar with King's "Letter from a Birmingham Jail." It's part of a multi-cultural education nowadays. What students may not know or pay attention to was the composition of the audience to whom King was writing: clergymen arguing the party line of gradualism, the idea that King should not insist on justice immediately, but over a period of time acceptable to the dominant power structure. In short, the clergy were ratifying injustice. King refused to accommodate them, arguing that they were the problem rather than the solution. It was a similar argument to the one Jesus leveled at the Pharisees. Neither argument received much support at the time.[1]

That's the essence, I suspect, of what it means to be a real priest: never feeling entirely comfortable with one's own kind because, if you do, then you've given away the sharp-edged sword needed to cut away hypocrisy and illusion. Both King and Jesus were perceived as enemies by those pretending to be friends. It couldn't be any other way if they were to serve the Lord in truth. Their detractors would predictably accuse them of having other agendas. Neither King nor Jesus withered under the assault.

Someone might argue that I'm being unfair by insisting that all priests ought to have the moral courage of King or Jesus. I'm inclined to ask "Then, what's a priest for?" But I do understand the point only too well. Few of us possess the vision or strength to love fearlessly. For that reason, I will continue to pray for all of those who serve in their official roles as priests. Why would I want any less for them than for anyone else struggling along the path? There's an old prayer, one that acknowledges the difficulties they face and one I now offer on their behalf:

> Prayer for Priests
>
> Keep them, I pray Thee, dearest Lord, keep them, for they are Thine—Thy priests whose lives burn out before Thy consecrated shrine.
>
> Keep them, for they are in the world, though from the world apart; When earthly pleasures tempt, allure—shelter them in Thy heart.
>
> Keep them, and comfort them in hours of loneliness and pain, when all their lives of sacrifice for souls seems but in vain.
>
> Keep them, and O remember, Lord, they have no one but Thee, yet they have only human hearts, with human frailty.
>
> Keep them as spotless as the Host, that daily they caress; their every thoughts and word and deed, Deign, dearest Lord, to bless.
>
> Our Father ... Hail Mary ... Glory Be ...[2]

1. King, *Strength to Love*, 3–162.
2. "Prayer for Priests," Catholic Online.

Psalm 133

"Behold, how good and pleasant it is for brethren to dwell together in unity." (Ps 133:1)

I mean it quite literally when I say there are people who relish the current culture wars and the disunity they engender. These people profit from being self-appointed ideologues and "defenders" of morality. It doesn't seem to matter what they do in their personal lives. The trickle-down effect of their poison is disastrous, reinforcing insensitivity and self-absorption in abundance. Once we understood these qualities to be undesirable and dangerous. Now we legitimatize them, pointing out how indispensable they are in the global marketplace where losers too often lack the killer instinct. Somehow we are able to overlook the flaws in this line of reasoning, promoting instead a mindless cultural mythology that ours is the greatest country on earth. We silence all efforts suggesting a balanced view and deride anyone who tries to engage in the sort of critical thinking that really is the hallmark of a great country. Because the young have no memory of what they've never experienced, they do not know that it was ever any other way than it is now. I have students who consider it their right to have a loaded AK-47 in their homes. A right? Perhaps. But does anyone stop to ask what such a nonchalant acceptance of our own violent tendencies says about us? Since when did we begin to enshrine ignorance and condescension, narrowness of intellect, and lack of respect for other people? It is a lonely world for those who oppose these things, especially when the overwhelming majority of others put forth their platform of divisiveness in the name of Christ. Has God's name ever been so misused or abused?

Occasionally one finds a voice of truth in the wilderness. Such a voice came to me in a book I was reading the other day. The author, Robert Jensen, had this to say about the post 9/11 world:

> I have never been more distant from my peers. I have never felt so fundamentally alone so often. The community in which I feel comfortable has shrunk dramatically. When in 'normal' settings, such as work, I usually feel as if I live in some parallel universe. I find myself more frequently communicating over e-mail with like-minded people in other cities rather than chatting with colleagues in the hallway. Instead of looking for ways to expand my social circle, I have let it contract.[1]

There is no reason to pretend I don't feel this way, and from conversations with others around the country I know that many feel similarly. The United States has taken an ugly turn since 9/11. Decent people shouldn't feel alienation, nor can we wallow in a sense of being different. We must not separate ourselves from the larger world that creates this sense of being alone. If we do that—if those who want to resist the American empire cut ourselves off from the larger society—it will be the ultimate privilege.

At the moment, it seems that corporate sponsorship of all life on the planet is the ultimate goal of those in positions of social and political power. The kindest gesture we can offer these people is not to assume they are sane. The Trinitarian god they worship is one indivisibly connected to money, technology, and domination of others. They do not see literally the consequences for the human community of idolizing these entities. Theirs is a tragic flaw that makes them blind to their own excesses and to the results of our collective obsession with greed. Never in our history, with the possible exception of the debate over slavery, has the country been so divided, offering small hope of recognizing the common good or participating in the blessings of the human family. How many people are willing to let go of their hatred and hostility in order to accept these blessings? How many of us have spent too much time nurturing our affection for these petty gods ever to let them go?

---

1. Jensen, *End of Patriarchy*, 101.

Psalm 134

"Behold, bless ye the Lord, all ye servants of the Lord, which by night stand in the house of the Lord." (Ps 134:1)

I like to think of them as guarding the four corners of my house: angels, flaming entities, all with names, all vigilant with full awareness of our comings and goings. They can travel at the speed of light, materializing anywhere at any time to protect us. And this is a world where we need all the protection we can get, where it seems we're always a hair-width away from danger.

Ours is the age of anxiety. Humanity fails to trust itself, fails to trust God. People barricade themselves behind the walls of their homes with all the conveniences and strategies of alienation that postmodern society affords. I actually heard a poet, of all people, say recently that her fantasy was to own a house without windows. It seems we'll do anything to stay locked up within ourselves. Remaining vulnerable is no longer viewed as a virtue but as the acme of foolishness. As a friend of mine confessed not long ago: "I don't trust anybody—not even you." His statement stunned me until I acknowledged that almost no one gives anyone the benefit of the doubt these days. Everything is contractual. Everything is for sale, including what passes for love. Under these circumstances, how we can even stand to be in each other's presence is a miracle. Better to keep our distance via cell phone. Better never to answer the call to adventure that invites us to a genuine discovery of ourselves and others.

We are a drain on each other, no doubt about it. People's lives (what they say and do) are so programmed, so routinized, as to be nauseatingly predictable. The result of this ennui is to entice us to go to sleep. In a culture of death, that seems the natural thing to do. But God calls us not to do the thing most natural and despairing. He wants us to lift the self-imposed burdens of our lives—the cross we bear unnecessarily—from our shoulders. It is because life is so precious that we're afraid of losing it.

That's why I take comfort that, despite my fears, I have supernatural assistance in combating natural tendencies and obstacles that keep me from being brave on behalf of God. That means remaining open to possibilities of life even in the midst of so much manufactured and advertised death. As children of light, we are pilgrims, wayfarers, people destined to find our home elsewhere. But we are also promised protection for the journey. Mine comes in the form of what I imagine to be persons of light, speed, and love. For my part, I want to make them as welcome here as I can.

Psalm 135

"The idols of the heathen are silver and gold, the work of men's hands. They have mouths, but they speak not; eyes have they, but they see not; They have ears, but they hear not; neither is there any breath in their mouths. They that make them are like unto them: so is every one that trusteth in them." (Ps 135:15–18)

A culture of acquisition and narrow self-interest—that's what we've opted for. Just yesterday I heard from a friend, a successful business person and someone I've known since childhood. I try to maintain a connection with him, but it's hard. We might as well be shouting at each other across the Atlantic Ocean, so vast is the gulf between us. I don't think he's even aware of the extent to which everything he says and does revolves around what he owns or can buy. His is a world of resume building, BMWs, private schools, country clubs, and gated communities. Nothing else matters or is considered real if it exists outside this diaspora of wealth.

My friend has never done anything in his adult life for which the cash nexus isn't in the forefront of his transactions. He married a trophy wife for the money and family connections she could offer. He lives in increasingly upscale neighborhoods with his kind of people, and he defends his right to do that.

More telling, perhaps, is what he doesn't do. He doesn't do anything for which there isn't an ostensible monetary reward or a return on current investments. He doesn't do any sort of service to the community that isn't some form of public relations or self-advertising. Even his charity work is designed to put the firm he runs in a good light. Finally, he doesn't know anyone who isn't rich or white with the exception of childhood chums, and he doesn't understand how anyone could want it any other way.

It would probably hurt his feelings to know I'd pointed out these things about him. But in many ways, he's an easy person to placate. All you have to do is listen to him. He'll do all the talking. And the talk will center on what SUV he just bought, what vacation he's taking, what top-drawer schools his children attend, what celebrity he met on the plane last week . . .

Psalm 136

"... for his mercy endureth forever." (Ps 136:2)

The above phrase acts as a refrain in each of the 26 verses of this psalm. It is a reminder of what we too often take for granted. Truth told, the ancient Israelites didn't want mercy for their *enemies*. In the context we find here, *mercy* paradoxically describes the way God favored his people by destroying their opponents. Failing to do that, God would have been perceived as anything but a merciful protector. We do well to recall that the sort of God the Israelites wanted was a destroyer, an avenger. They awaited a Messiah who would usher in a reign of terror. The Bible describes it as a *joy* to see one's enemies put to rout.

If we are honest with ourselves, we must conclude that, like the people of the Old Testament, we'd prefer to have a wrathful God, one willing to take up the justness of our cause. In fact, we automatically assume our cause to be just. We find it offensive, reprehensible, that God would extend mercy to our enemies whoever we perceive them to be. We demand justice and feel justified in doing so. Mercy is an offense to the justice to which we are entitled.

Insisting on this state of circumstances is unfortunate because it compels us, sooner or later, to confront an essential question: Where is the justice of the cross? It is nowhere to be found. Only mercy resides there. Jesus' death on the cross destroyed all claims of justice and crucified all desires for revenge. Thus, God has every right to say "Vengeance is mine" and to cancel all our insistent claims of justice.

Jesus came to correct our view of God, infuriating people in the process. He emphasizes how we can't insist on justice and at the same time expect to receive mercy. In the parable of the prodigal son, he focuses not so much on the dissolute son as on his self-righteous brother, the loyal one who wants to see his profligate sibling punished. The father reminds his angry son that both he and his lost brother are precious to him. The implication is that the father would be just as merciful if the situation were reversed.

Mercy is the opposite of justice. It's that simple. And woe be unto those who insist, like the angry brother in the parable, on being right and demanding restitution. Only a self-imposed and perpetual blindness can keep them from seeing that their time will come, time when holding onto justice will condemn them. The lesson of Jesus's life is that God does not condemn us. We do that all by ourselves by insisting on standards of rightness (i.e., righteousness) that, like cruel gods in every age, delight in our failures. A loving God would protect us from the shame of our all-too-human mistakes. A loving God would celebrate the change of heart by which, once being dead, we are now alive.

Psalm 137

"O daughter of Babylon, who art to be destroyed; happy shall he be, that rewardeth thee as thou hast served us." (Ps 137:8)

My mother hated men; therefore, she hated me. That is a difficult admission to make. Only after years of prayer, self-reflection, and therapy can I make it. No one wants to confess to being unloved or unlovable. It requires acknowledging an extraordinary amount of damage done to oneself. A person has to rise up out of the rubble of his or her own being.

I once read that it's biologically impossible for children to accept the fact that they aren't loved. To do that would result in a meltdown of the child's personality—even his or her soul. So we invent elaborate defense mechanisms and create rationalizations early on, repressing what we can't bear to accept. Only, these things can't last forever. When the truth starts to break to the surface of consciousness, our protective mechanisms, no longer as effective as they once were, refuse to let us live with the illusions we've created. Indeed, as an adult, I could no longer ignore the animosity my mother had for me or the cruel things she said to me in my early years. She later regretted much of what passed between us. That did not mitigate the harm resulting from what she said. To this day, I have no trouble sniffing out the difference between guilt and love. They are two distinctly different odors.

Nor am I certain what it means to agree to forgive a person who feels bad about hating you. I prefer a person's rejection of me to be of purer ore and without the qualifications that made someone feel better about herself for feeling as she does. Lies told in order to be *nice* only confuse. By contrast, the truth will set you free, just as the Bible says.

I do feel a huge sadness that my mother was made to feel so conflicted and guilty about being created in the feminine image of God. For Genesis makes it clear that God created man in his own image, both *male* and *female*. Our bodies are not objects to despise or to be exploited by others. Instead, we should experience a sense of joy about bodies, sex, and the gift of sharing.

My mother rightfully chafed at having the most powerful gift at her disposal abused and belittled. But she came to hate the gift itself. I understand her inclination. Her life and faith were taken from her at a tender age. I have a picture of her, standing by a rose bush at about age ten, looking for all the world like a concentration camp victim. No one recognized her suffering. Few today seem to realize the extent to which our misunderstanding and improper teaching of Christian dogma result in a culture of alienation, eroticized violence, and death. What a sad legacy we have created in the name of God!

Lest anyone think this is exclusively a woman's predicament, let me put a finer edge on it. Because my mother viewed her own body and sexuality as shameful, she rejected my own burgeoning manhood, teasing me about my girlfriends, reading notes and letters I received, and haranguing me about the consequences of getting some *slut* pregnant. If she wasn't going to be happy in her body, I wasn't going to be happy in mine.

Over the years I've seen less virulent manifestations of these behaviors in women I've known. It makes me wonder why men never stop to ask why the women around them are sometimes controlling, bitchy, or seemingly impossible to please. In such a culture, how could they be anything else? Also, my entire adult life, I've been seeking to please an unpleasable ghost—that of my mother—by tallying up professional accomplishments and being *good* in all the ways society deems valuable. I have not reflected enough on the damage this compulsion may have cause me and those I love.

Now I am in the process of reexamining my approach to what I need to be doing to please myself and the God who violates even our sacred canons about him. I no longer desire to be *good* or to please people whose psychic damage makes them unpleasable. It is enough to set them free by doing what I need in order to answer a call to adventure that is life and faith affirming. I can think of no greater gift to give them.

Psalm 138

"The Lord will perfect that which concerneth me ..." (Ps 138:8)

As a child, I was a stick warrior in the light-mottled woods that served as my undisputed kingdom. To be alone in those acres and acres of tall trees and dense undergrowth that bordered our home was, though unknown to me at the time, one of the genuine spiritual experiences of my life. All the more for not being called that, for having no name at all.

As an only child, I learned early how to entertain myself. I enjoy my own company, knowing that if I talk to myself, I'm required to hear what I have to say. Of course, all was not as silent as it seemed. If I actually perched on a rock or stump and waited for a while, I'd begin to detect all sorts of *presences*. Birdsong, usually a cacophony as opposed to a euphony of sounds, was evidence of that. The shadow of a buzzard overhead or a sleepy night owl still hugging a branch in the early morning gave me all the proof I needed that I was not alone. Squirrels, too, materialized, chasing each other in insane joy, first on the ground, then in the awaiting oaks and hickories. Beetles and ant squadrons carried on more pedestrian business at my feet.

It was before the time I owned as many words as I have to describe such things. It was before I became a story teller because the story was still being told to me. Nor did I sense anything I was inclined to call God in that place and time. That is to say, I felt no *other* but only what I myself was part of.

At this point in my life, with all its concepts and rituals and habits of despair, I feel it is a sin to be joyless. If the woods taught me anything, they taught me how to listen to what didn't require a name, to what made no demands at all, to what offered only an invitation. Anything else was assuredly not of God.

Mystical mumbo-jumbo? Perhaps. But later on, in the evening, I'd materialize out of the shadows and make my way to a rusted swing set onto whose frame I'd climb, pausing to stare at a furiously setting sun sinking from view. Only when its blood streaks remained did I feel something rising from depths incomprehensible to me. It was a single whispered word: *home*.

Psalm 139

"If I ascend up into heaven, thou art there; if I make my bed in hell, behold, thou art there." (Ps 139:8)

In a culture where the value is on doing, getting, and having, the idea of simply *being* is anathema to most people. Even now I'm involved in so many good causes, I can scarcely breathe: a peace institute, a group wanting to reform the Catholic Church, a civility campaign at work. All someone has to do is ask me. I'm so afraid of letting people down, I'll consent to carry the cross for almost any noble cause.

In fact, my entire sense of worth is bound up in what I do for other people, and I can never do enough. My identity is attached to action, activity, and helping. The reason is that at core I don't believe I'm worth much unless I'm achieving something. Not doing might render me anonymous, even invisible. And I would have to confront my own nothingness. I would be a naught, a cipher, a thing of no use. Even now I spend a lot of time grieving that some of my functions, ones that gave my life profound meaning, have ended or been transformed. Once I was the father of children; now I am the father of three adults. So much of my identity was bound up in being the earlier sort of father. The grief at losing the person I used to be is almost unspeakable. Rather than face this change, I've gotten lost in causes and activities as compensation for changes that force me to re-evaluate my identity. I'm working hard to avoid the specter of worthlessness—the dragon born in my childhood and stalking me all my life.

Some part of me knows I have to confront the beast, or it will kill me. Like many men my age, I've already surrendered to some of its manifestations: alcoholism, workaholism, perfectionism, not to mention the joylessness that eventually results in strokes, heart attacks, and cancer. Obviously, my strategies as a warrior have let me play into the enemy's hands too many times.

I need to detach from the stress cycle that threatens both body and spirit. I need to pray for help in making me a more savvy opponent—one wise as a serpent, but innocent of obsessions and compulsions and the need for constant validation. My life depends on what I'm unable to accomplish by myself. If only I were willing to let God do for me what needs doing without my perpetual interference.

Psalm 140

"Deliver me, O Lord, from the evil man." (Ps 140:1)

I was napping on the sofa last night and woke to a documentary on prison life in one particularly hard-core facility in California. This one houses gang leaders representing the spectrum of ethnic groups in America, as well as many of the institutionalized hatred prevalent throughout the country. In prison, apparently, those hatreds exist in their purest and most virulent forms. Almost everyone was schooled in techniques of terror to which few of us are ever exposed.

Make no mistake. These individuals are beyond the pale, scarcely human, one might say. I confess I was glad they were quarantined with their own kind, an admission that puts me in a compromising situation, on the one hand, while revealing my naiveté on the other. If only evil could be so easily contained.

At one point in the documentary, a prisoner was strip-searched and found to contain in one of his body cavities a coded list of more than six hundred names of people on the outside, many of them women and children, targeted for hits. Obviously prison walls offer no protection from people bent on exercising their will at the expense of others. Indeed, those walls pose no obstacles at all to gang leaders and drug lords who honestly see little difference in being inside prison or out. Their lives are not altered significantly either way. In fact, some criminals don't mind the inconvenience of prison because prison itself is just another conduit, a thoroughfare for crime. Imagine being equally at home behind bars or in the streets. Imagine seeing no qualitative difference between the two. Every place the same.

Jesus was convicted and executed as a criminal. Paul gave shape to Christian doctrine from a prison cell, the closest thing to hell on earth any of us can imagine. I understand the message: There are no walls God can't break down. But I also know that the peculiar alchemy of personal and institutional evil creates intolerable fear, giving rise to calculated hatreds and suffering of indescribable proportions. I've further come to realize there's no such thing as safety or a safe place. As John Milton says, we're inclined to "make a heav'n of hell or a hell of heav'n."[1] The anxiety comes from knowing how easily we can turn one into the other.

1. Milton, *Paradise Lost*.

Psalm 141

"Our bones are scattered at the grave's mouth, as when one cutteth and cleaveth wood upon the earth." (Ps 141:7)

If I hadn't known better, I'd have sworn the young woman was experiencing delirium tremens. Her eyes danced, her foot shook, and at one point she stood and bounced on the balls of her feet like a boxer awaiting the next round.

What was producing such agitation? Brittany is a student in my American literature class, and we were working in small groups, preparing for a kind of College Bowl competition among students taking the course. Brittany and her group had studied 20 minutes, and now she was "bored." I wanted to tell her that she didn't know enough to be bored; and that as long as there was something to learn, she had no need to let the word slip into her lexicon. I resisted, realizing she'd only perceive such scolding as evidence of a misplaced and fusty concern for the general condition of the young. Besides, she'd probably forgotten to take her Ritalin, and as everyone knows, Ritalin is as indispensable to the current youth culture as Prozac is to its parents. No need to appear sanctimonious about Generation X when we oldsters have our own problems.

But I was disturbed, nonetheless, if for no other reason but the young woman seemed close to cachexia, as if her body couldn't help surrendering to a need for stimulation. What was the origin of such a need? I suspect it can be found in a phenomenon puzzling one cultural observer as follows:

> The puzzle is why so many people live so badly. No so wickedly, but so inanely. Not so cruelly, but so stupidly. There is little to admire and less to imitate in the people who are prominent in our culture. We have celebrities but not saints. Famous entertainers amuse a nation of bored insomniacs. Infamous criminals act out the aggressions of timid conformists. Petulant and spoiled athletes

play games vicariously for lazy and apathetic spectators. People, aimless and bored, amuse themselves with trivia and trash. Neither the adventure of goodness nor the pursuit of righteousness gets headlines.[1]

According to the dictionary, the word *boredom* is a relatively new addition to the language. It would be interesting to know to what extent the word's frequency corresponds to the regular use of the word's *amusement*, *technology*, and *distraction*. Surely some sort of meaningful connection exists among these words to explain the meaninglessness of our times.

As for the young woman who displayed all the tics associated with St. Vitus's dance, I can only pray that she and we don't succumb to terminal boredom and endless distraction, failing to notice or even care when "our bones are scattered at the grave's mouth."

---

1. Peterson, *Run/Horses*.

Psalm 142

"When my spirit was overwhelmed within me, then thou knewest my path." (Ps 142:3)

During the Middle Ages, the French theologian Abelard was condemned as a heretic for teaching, among other things, that God's love extended to all people, not just those accepting Jesus. For many Christians, Abelard received what he deserved. After all, Christian dogma evolved along strict lines emphasizing that Jesus saves only those who believe in him. Such a view has given rise to widespread meanness taking various forms, such as the Inquisition, anti-Semitism, and vicious nationalism. One wonders what Jesus would have thought of all these atrocities engineered in his name. On the other hand, Jesus says he came with a sword, and he has plenty to say about those who fail to take his teachings seriously. He has no trouble identifying both the hard-hearted and the hard-headed, and he offers stiff warnings to both. "Woe unto you" is a phrase of chilling condemnation that Jesus invokes with considerable frequency.

What's interesting, however, are the people to whom he directs this language. They are almost invariably the lawgivers, the scribes, and Pharisees, who extract a pound of flesh from others while requiring nothing of themselves. Jesus makes clear that self- righteousness, rigidity, and religious exactitude are these people's reward. The fact that they set themselves apart from those around him is evidence of their separation from God.

Ironically, in choosing Jesus, we choose not to judge or cut ourselves away from the mass of humanity lost and stumbling in the wilderness. Jesus never condemns lost sheep. That is clear from everything he says. It is also clear that he is speaking for God, who insists paradoxically on giving us as wide a berth as possible in finding him. This paradox can be elaborated further: Jesus offers the one way that sanctifies all the other ways that enable us to come to God. If we stop to think about it, it can't be otherwise. Jesus didn't die for a select and deserving few. His whole ministry opposed this idea.

Instead, he crucified our judgmental natures, self-righteousness, and love of divisiveness, ensuring that these states of being died with him on the cross. He stretched out his arms, embracing the entire world. If this had not been the case, then God's love would be half-hearted and conditional, no different from that displayed by the Pharisees in his day or our own. Yet, what isn't always clear is that we're all Pharisees—blind, ignorant, and undeserving of a love we can scarcely conceive, a love that negates itself by favoring some over others. My proof? A medieval monk named Abelard found himself excommunicated from the church because he dared assert that God loves us not just in spite of our faults, but because of them. For many people, this proposition is just too distasteful to believe.

Psalm 143

"And enter not into judgment with thy servant: for in thy sight shall no living man be justified." (Ps 143:2)

My father lied for me once. To my everlasting surprise, he told a lie to keep me from experiencing a shameful circumstance. An honorable man who sought to be upright and truthful in all his dealings, he was nonetheless willing to violate his own code in order to keep me from hanging on the cross longer than necessary. He knew I was guilty, but he was willing to break his own law and to be an accomplice in my crime in order to demonstrate his love for me. Still, if you'd asked him, he wouldn't have acknowledged what he was doing. Nor did he use the occasion to assert his moral superiority or to deliver a lecture, making an example of me.

If you expect me to say that the most important gleanings I learned from this incident were rectitude and probity, then you'll be disappointed. I don't care a damn about those things as abstractions. What changed my life was not that I was held to an impossibly high standard, but that I wasn't. Indeed, my father's love and merciful concern for me canceled out any requirements of righteousness he might have entertained. Like Jesus, he crucified the law, making it no longer applicable and excusing me in the process.

From that time on, I've tried to be aware that being liars one and all, we don't need to point too stern a finger at others. Why? Not one of us is worthy to have someone else bear the brunt of our deceptions, but in our heart of hearts, that's what we hope for. We hope that Jesus will take our place on the cross. This desire is our sorry confession—that we're willing to let Jesus stand in for us to avoid the shame, ridicule, and alienation our sins invite. Jesus dies in scandal so we won't be scandalized.

I was ecstatic the day my father lied. Only later did I soberly consider the cost to him or what a gift he'd given me. He never mentioned it. But it was one of the transforming events of my life and is transforming me even as I write about it. My nature is to be self-righteous. I only hope that like my father I can find the love in me to make an excuse for someone undeserving so as not to let that person hang on the cross a moment longer than necessary.

Psalm 144

"Lord, what is man that thou takest knowledge of him or the son of man that though makest account of him!" (Ps 144:3)

Jesus was an outlaw. Although he claimed he'd come to fulfill the law, the narrow minds around him found all the ways he broke it. From their point of view, they had plenty of evidence to convict him. No wonder Jesus warned of lawyers and their airtight cases.

I see it every day: good little boys and girls feeling justified in being about everybody's business but their own. They are bean counters who uphold a sham morality and its vicious legalism while never once considering the Law of Love that makes all other laws unnecessary. That's right! This law takes care of them all.

Good little boys and girls don't want to believe that precept. It simultaneously makes circumstances both too easy and too hard. And it robs these special folks of the job of feeling good about themselves. I have a theory that if Jesus returned today, these people would have perfectly good reasons for putting him to death, while making his life miserable as hell.

Speaking of hell, Jesus makes clear that we choose it for ourselves by opting for law over life and love. Indeed, I have no doubt that hell will be an efficient and well-run organization. Its management will have clear guidelines and policy statements so everyone will know exactly what's expected. People who found this arrangement satisfactory in life will have no trouble adjusting in the hereafter. Failure to adhere to the corporate agenda might land someone in another place altogether.

Jesus, ever the fool, rejected Satan's corporate enticements of wealth and power. To accept those offerings meant becoming part of an exclusive club with its own rules for admission. Jesus resisted being what he was expected to be by those in charge, by the minions who devise ambitious plans for the rest of us and rules to ensure that we remain within the circle of their influence. Stepping beyond that circle, Jesus brought down upon himself the wrath of the lawgivers. As always, the good little boys and girls were there to tally all the rules he'd broken and to see to it that he was punished with all the expedient fury and self-righteousness their hard-little hearts could muster. After all, they were right; he was wrong.

The law makes no excuses for anybody. Jesus, in his great abiding love, made excuses for everyone. For those who had no excuses, he let himself be the ultimate excuse. Only someone who was the fulfillment of love could risk doing that. Only those insisting on adherence to rules could fail to see what he had done.

Psalm 145

"The Lord is good to all; and his tender mercies are over all his works."
(Ps 145:9)

I sometimes mention to my students that if they want to read a quest narrative—that is, a story in which a character sets out to find another—they don't need to look any further than the couple of pages comprising the book of Jonah, tucked neatly between Obadiah and Micah. There is, however, one significant difference between Jonah and other archetypal heroes. Jonah fails to answer the call to adventure and, as a result, finds himself in a worse spot than if he'd obeyed God's summons and gone to Nineveh in the first place. In fact, his is a kind of default quest. By refusing one journey, he's forced to take another.

Most people have a general idea of what happens to Jonah. He flees his country by booking passage on a ship soon tossed about in a tempest. Suspecting Jonah has something to do with raging seas, the sailors heave him overboard whereupon a great fish swallows him up. Jonah spends three days and nights in the fish's belly—a precursor to Christ's spending the same span of time in the tomb—and, after much praying, is burped up on land. Surely, the story has to be the greatest fish tale ever told. Neither *Moby Dick* nor Hemingway's *The Old Man and the Sea* can hold a candle to it.

But all this adventure—or misadventure—eclipses the most important part of the tale, which happens afterward. After being rescued, Jonah doggedly sets out to Nineveh to fulfill his original mission. Still unhappy about having to make the trip, he strikes a deal with God: if the people of Nineveh fail to repent, then God will strike them dead without delay.

Jonah preaches till he's hoarse but to no avail. He perches atop a hill and calls upon God to keep his promise. God shows up, essentially saying he's changed his mind and has decided to spare the sinners in the city below. Jonah cries foul. Once God has made up his mind, He's not supposed to change it! God says he can change his mind if he wants to as long as such a change results in mercy.

Recognizing Jonah's peevishness and frustration, God sidles up to him, trying to make a case of the "tender mercies" mentioned by the Psalmist. In so many words, God implores him. "Jonah, do you really want me to destroy six score thousand people who don't know their left hand from their right? Besides, what about the cattle? Do you want me to kill them too?"

What's interesting is how the book ends with a question, the only book in the Bible that does. Either we're to assume that God is being rhetorical and Jonah knows it, or the more likely scenario is that Jonah hasn't learned a single thing despite what's happened to him. Either way, the author of the book of Jonah mercifully decides to give God the final word.

Psalm 146

"The Lord preserveth the strangers; he relieveth the fatherless and widow." (Ps 146:9)

I listened to a homily on Sunday in which the priest extolled the local Right to Life people for standing on the street corner, passing out literature, and seeking donations. He noted, in particular, the courage displayed by these folks. I began to think about that when a quotation by French philosopher Gabriel Marcel popped into my head: "Fidelity is the opposite of conformity."[2] That put the whole notion of the Right to Life group's "courage" into sharp relief. If courage is what we're seeking, then the real courage would have been that shown by those on the other side of the issue had they chosen to stand on the same street corner. Living in a part of the country where almost everyone believes in the right to life, they would have been the ones to receive snubs, taunts, and threats. And the people hurling objections at them would feel justified. Courageous fanaticism is still fanaticism.

I believe that I am on the side of life. It's just that I'm not always on the side of those who say they're on the side of life. To tell the truth, many of them feel too good about themselves. They believe they're heroes and seem never to have a moment's doubt or anxiety. If there's one thing I've learned in these 50 years, it's that if you feel that what you're doing is unqualifiedly right, then you're probably doing something wrong.

Do I wish that women didn't receive abortions? Absolutely. Indeed, I wish that we all worked ceaselessly to create a world in which it would never occur to people to have abortions. That would be a world in which children were welcome and cherished and cared for with all the resources at our disposal. All children—not just white children or affluent children

---

2. Marcel, *Creative Fidelity*, 154.

or American children—though there are plenty of the latter abandoned by society almost at the instant they're born. That's because many of those same people clamoring for a right to life also oppose taxes or other financial support that would guarantee adequate health care or equality of education for all our children.

The church isn't beyond implicating itself in this state of matter either. The same priest touting the courage of the pro-life demonstrators refused to respond to a letter I wrote him about substantiated instances of clerical sexual abuse involving children in our diocese. In the eleventh hour, he canceled an appointment with me, leaving a message on my answering machine saying he'd received a free ticket to see *The Passion of the Christ*. If I thought about the irony of that long enough, I might just pull the covers over my head and call it a day.

No one doubts the need for courage. But it seems to me that authentic courage enables us to confront our own contradictions and shortcomings in a spirit of humility, recognizing that we're not always able to feel good about who we are or what we do. Being on the cross is never comfortable; but it may be inevitable if we are to learn how to face the fear and indifference that keep us from appreciating the stranger, the widow or widower, and the fatherless and motherless—people closest, God says, to his own heart.

Psalm 147

"The Lord lifteth up the meek: he casteth the wicked down to the ground." (Ps 147:6)

Yesterday I had the honor of attending an awards ceremony for students in the Developmental Studies program at my college. This program is designed to help those who are academically unprepared to enroll in college-level courses. The two women professors who arranged the ceremony wanted to recognize students who aren't accustomed to receiving much recognition. Among them were a young man who'd had a paralyzing stroke, a single mother who'd raised her child in shelters and on the street, and a shy young woman who'd been forced to leave her family in Africa. All were grateful for the certificates and the accolades they received, shedding tears in some cases and applauding enthusiastically for their peers. No hint of envy or peevishness could be detected. Each knew what obstacles the others had overcome. Sitting there, I was overwhelmed by the realization that it often takes precious little to make a difference in a person's life and that the people I was seeing were the meek our Lord speaks of loving. They are the overlooked and discarded, those considered a burden by the more confident and successful, the minions who clamor about the necessity of contributing to society but who make contributions mainly to themselves. I'm content to let this latter group bask in their self-manufactured glory. They are, after all, their own reward.

As for the first group, so often pushed to the brink and beyond, I glimpsed the Christ Heartedness and Christ Woundedness we are all destined to share. As they stepped shyly onto that small stage, their joy was undeniable, and I for one was happy to be the recipient of a grace that found me in their presence.

Psalm 148

"Praise the Lord from the earth, ye dragons, and all deeps." (Ps 148:7)

This psalm unites the field theory of all creation, revealing the peaceable kingdom that is both God's promise and one of his greatest blessings. There is an almost Celtic quality to these verses, a charm that derives from an awareness that all categories of creation, whether flower, mineral, plant, animal, or human being, are linked to the loving consciousness of God who brings them into being by his divine word, or *Logos*.

At one level, all of these creations contribute to an underlying harmony, a great peace and stability reflective of a pure consciousness of love. How could it be otherwise? And yet, our Fall, our descent into the lower worlds of awareness, these spiritual blunders result in much damage and frightening occurrences in the physical plane of existence. What the ancients knew that we don't seem to comprehend is that violence at this level translates into distortions on the spiritual plane. How many times does Jesus warn us not to be deceived by appearances? What we see is not all there is to see. The present, time-bound reality is not the Reality. But the realm of timelessness, the peaceable kingdom, is affected by what we do in the here and now.

How many souls are seeking to be born into this life space so they can begin their spiritual ascent? Given our distortions of consciousness, however, we often fail to grasp that by preventing these souls entrance into this plane or by refusing to nurture them once they're here, we do untold cosmic damage.

All creation is unfolding. All creation is connected. Our thought structure and fear mechanisms keep us from seeing. Not even death is the end but only the beginning of the next step in our development, in the process of co-creation by which every human being participates in becoming like Jesus. He is the consciousness of love in which all creation is united and which God is made manifest in all:

> Mountains and all hills; fruitful trees and all cedars:
> Beasts and all cattle; creeping things and flying fowl:
> Kings of the earth and all people: princes and all the judges of the earth:
> Both young men, and maidens; old men, and children:
> Let them praise the name of the Lord: for his name alone is excellent;
> his glory is above the earth and heaven.

Psalm 149

"Let the high praises of God be in their mouth and a two edged sword in their hand." (Ps 149:6)

I never considered comparing the archetypal philosopher to Jesus, but here the comparison seems to pertain. It seems to me more and more that the philosopher, as a necessary man of tomorrow and the day after tomorrow, has always found himself, and always had to find himself in opposition to his today: the ideal of the day was always his enemy. Hitherto all these promoters of the human, who are called philosophers, and who rarely have felt themselves to be friends of wisdom, but rather disagreeable fools and dangerous question marks, have found their tasks, their hard, unwanted, incapable task, in being the bad conscious of their time.

Jesus opposed the virtuous men of his time. Living within a self-created system, they believed they had all the answers, assigning those answers sacred status. They believed they had solved the puzzle of man, closing the door on further possibilities of becoming.

Yet, Jesus flung open the door, insisting that He'd come to show men and women another way to live. Jesus dared to suggest that our humanity was, in reality, divinity, and that a new paradigm of reality was required, one as radical as the shift from Newtonian physics to Quantum theory. Calling himself the Son of Man, he understood his role perfectly. He was a new kind of being, one to which the rest of us could aspire to evolve. This new being lived beyond categories of virtue designed to condemn some and praise others. Instead, Jesus promised to show us how to cut loose from old styles and beliefs, how to have a new consciousness of ourselves that enables us to create new realities and revel in the energy of existence. He said that if we could adopt this consciousness, then we would see how we already live in the Absolute and that the kingdom of God is truly "at hand."

Unfortunately, few believed him or understood the power in what he said. Even in his own time, few wished to believe or had the courage to declare that Jesus is the sort of being we are all destined to become and could be even now if we chose to surrender our limited conceptions of ourselves and the notion that God exists apart from us. The original sin, as Jesus observes, was not in thinking we were like God, but in thinking we weren't while insisting on pulling away from our divine natures. Jesus came to tell us that such separation was an illusion. Our present "reality" is anything but real, as mystics like Eckhart, St. Francis, and St. Teresa of Avila have maintained.

Organized Christianity finds such an idea appalling and heretical, falling into the very trap Jesus warned about. Thus, the church frequently lapses into sin by emphasizing the predicament of the old Adam rather than acknowledging its evolutionary calling in proclaiming us new creatures the way Jesus is and was. Indeed, the church is fearful of such a claim. Hence, its theology erects barriers, identifying Jesus with a distant, hammer-fist of a God; dividing our flesh from our spirit; and making salvation a longed-for desire when Jesus tells us we are free from the effects of sin if we only believe we are free. Our belief that sin binds us keeps us bound to sin. The church makes sure that it is needed in its present form by reminding us how sinful and death-bound we are, even though Christ tells us that is not the case. If we had the faith to understand Jesus's words and if that faith permeated every molecule of our beings, then we could move mountains and raise the dead, just as the Scripture tells us.

By the authority of God, Jesus at one point asks his disciples, "Are ye not Gods?" thereby reminding them of their divine natures and giving them a glimpse of the new "kingdom," a mode of consciousness that transcends the second law of thermodynamics, which insists that all life is subject to entropy, decay, and dissolution. This fatalistic scenario isn't valid, Jesus insists but is a manifestation of the illusion that clouds our awareness, preventing us from accepting our rightful inheritance as divine sons and daughters.

Nor is this inheritance something we have to earn. It is an immutable fact of our existence in God, which is another way of saying God exists immutably in us. The evil comes in denying our true natures, insisting that the illusion is real and even making it a foundational support of our theology. And while it is true that at one level, the level of bifurcated consciousness, hell is woefully real, at another level—the level of union with our divine selves—hell ceases to exist the instant we deny its reality.

Psalm 150

"Praise him with the sound of the trumpet: praise him with the psaltery and harp." (Ps 150:3)

My father used to say he couldn't carry a tune in a bucket. Neither can I. I can't toot a horn, strike a drum, or pluck stringed instruments. It's not that I don't like music. I do. I have enormous admiration for people who can lift our hearts to the heavens with their songs.

Mark Twain shared my lack of musical ability. Only he was a bit more peevish about being denied this singular talent. Acknowledging that not one in ten thousand people on earth can play the harp, Twain observed that apparently all of us will be expected to play this instrument once we arrive in heaven.[1] Obviously, for Twain, words served as music, and his tones ranged from lighthearted to solemn, bitter to sublime.

Whatever else we can say about music, it is a divine gift. Who knows, maybe those of us who can't carry a tune in a bucket on this plane will be able to strike heavenly chords in the next world. Maybe we'll all develop the fine-tuned ear of the Lord who hears all sound as a symphony of creation—beloved in its groaning and delightful in every pip and squeak that rises in perpetual praise of the Creator.

---

1. Twain, *Letters*, 97.

Postface

I was preparing this book for publication when the pandemic struck hard. What soon became clear was that the entire planet was facing a peril not experienced in more than a century. The 1918 influenza pandemic spread world-wide during 1918 into 1919. Estimates indicate that about 500 million people, or one-third of the world's population, became infected with the H1N1 virus. Mortality rates were exacerbated by the lack of a vaccine and antibiotics to combat secondary bacterial infections. My reference to this earlier pandemic is not meant to diminish the horrors of COVID-19. It is simply to remind myself and my readers that plagues of one sort or another have afflicted humankind since the dawning of the ages.

Biblical plagues included water turning to blood, frogs, lice, flies, livestock pestilence, boils, hail, locusts, darkness, and the killing of first-born children. Most notably, of course, was the Black Plague, a devastating global epidemic of Bubonic plague striking Europe and Asia in the 1300s, killing between 30 and 60 percent of Europe's population. In absence of germ theory, the Black Death continued to be a scourge for more than three hundred years. In an age of increasing trade and travel, sailors were especially susceptible to the disease since boats harbored rats, and rats were infested with fleas carrying the bacillus bacteria, the source of the pandemic. Dock workers boarded ships often to discover most of the crew dead, and those still alive gravely ill and covered in black boils oozing blood and pus.

The Black Death was so much a fact of life in the fourteenth century that English author Geoffrey Chaucer and Italian writer Giovanni Boccaccio featured the plague as plot devices in their works. In the *Canterbury Tales*, Chaucer's Pardoner deems the plague fitting punishment for a trio of evil doers. Boccaccio's *Decameron* chronicles seven women and three men who flee the plague in Florence and hole up in a villa outside the city.

By the sixteenth century, the pestilential terrors of the Bubonic plague in England cast a dark cloud over Elizabethan society, making London, in particular, a Petri dish for successive waves of the disease. Nor was William Shakespeare unaware of a collective fear spreading through England almost as fast as the plague itself. Shakespeare's parents, a young couple in Stratford-upon-Avon, lost their first two children to the pandemic. The pair barricaded themselves inside their home to protect their three-month-old son, William, destined to become the greatest writer in the English-speaking world.

In adulthood, Shakespeare's life continued to be shaped by the plague, which he used as source material in his dramas. In the Bard's *Romeo and Juliette*, Romeo's cousin, Mercutio, who has received a mortal wound from the tip of a rapier wielded by a representative of a warring family, declares, "I am hurt. A plague o' both your houses!" Shakespeare was so fond of the word *plague* that he used it hundreds of times in his work.

As a literary historian, I examine the past's literature to find parallels with the present. What I understand is that trying to take the long view of an entity as terrifying as the current pandemic isn't likely to comfort anyone. Our situation is existentially unique to us. What history *can* do is underscore a fundamental reality that the terms of life don't change. Human beings will always face life and death challenges, however new they appear to successive generations.

Our questions won't likely find answers either, at least not satisfactory ones. One wonders whether God knows the outcome given the unstable equation human beings pose to their own survival through their fickle exercise of free will. It would be cause for despair but for a single promise revealed to all ages: God will suffer, like us, with us, as helpless as we would be if forced to witness the excruciating death of a child—our child.

God's grief, like ours, is the broken-hearted wailing that accompanies love lost and promises unfulfilled or broken. If God finds us in suffering, he refuses to leave us in darkness because Jesus has fulfilled all requirements of suffering and grief. In the Divine economy, he has sacrificed the necessary currency to earn his resurrection and ours: "If I am with you in suffering, then you will be with me in the joys of everlasting life." Jesus is the living embodiment of God's promise of love. If we struggle at times to retain that conviction, we only need to seek God's face in all its beauty and kaleidoscopic flux as a reflection of the ever changing sky.

Bibliography

Agee, James and Walker Evans. *Let Us Now Praise Famous Men*. New York: Houghton Mifflin, 1988.
Arendt, Hannah, quoted in Bernard Magnus. *The Cambridge Companion to Nietzsche*. Cambridge University Press, 1996. https://epdf.pub/the-cambridge-companion-to-nietzsche-cambridge-companions-to-philosophy.html.
Augustne of Hippo. *The Confessions of St. Augustine*. Ontario: Devoted Publishing, 1907.
Bauman, Zygmunt. *Liquid Love: On the Fragility of Human Bonds*. Maiden, MA: Polity, 2013.
Berman, Morris. *The Twilight of American Culture*. New York: W.W. Norton, 2001.
Berry, Wendell. "Word and Flesh." *What Are People For?* Berkeley: North Point, 1990.
Brewer, Cobham. *Brewer's Dictionary of Phrase and Fable*. Philadelphia: Henry Altemus, 1998.
Budde, Michael, and Robert Brimlow. *Christianity Incorporated*. Eugene, OR: Wipf and Stock, 2002.
Chodron, Pema. *Awakening Loving-Kindness*. Boston: Shambala, 2017.
Chuang Tzu. *The Way of Chuang Tzu*. Translated by Thomas Merton. Boston: NewDirections, 1969.
Coles, Robert. "Review of Cormac McCarthy's *Children of God*." *New Yorker* 50 (26 Aug. 1974): 87–90.
Comte-Sponville, Andre. *A Small Treatise on the Great Virtues*. New York: Macmillan, 2003.
Dawkins, Richard. "Harry Potter Fails to Cast Spell Over Richard Dawkins." *London Telegraph* (24 Oct. 2008): 18–19.
Dersiewicz, William. "Solitude and Leadership." *The American Scholar* (01 March 2010): 36–40.
Edwards, Jonathan. "Sinners in the Hands of an Angry God." *Norton Anthology of American Literature*. 9th ed., ed. N. Baym et al., 390–402. New York: W. W. Norton, 2017.
Elizabeth of the Trinity. "My Soul is a Heaven Where God Lives." Carmelite website. https://ocarm.org/en/.
Ellul, Jacques. *The Humiliation of the Word*. Grand Rapids: William B. Erdmanns, 1985.
Finley, James. *Christian Meditation*. San Francisco: Harper, 2004.
Florida, Richard. *The Rise of the Creative Class*. New York: Basic Books, 2002.
Foucault, Michel. *Society Must Be Defended*. New York: Macmillan, 2003.
Fox, Matthew. *Sins of the Spirit, Blessings of the Flesh*. New York: Three Rivers, 1999.

Bibliography

Frost, Robert. "After Apple Picking." Poetry Foundation. https://www.poetryfoundation.org/poems/44259/after-apple-picking.

———. "Stopping by Woods on a Snowy Evening." Poetry Foundation. https://www.poetryfoundation.org/poems/42891/stopping-by-woods-on-a-snowy-evening.

Frye, Northrop, quoted in Maynard Mack. *King Lear in Our Time*. Berkeley: Parallax, 2005.

Gilmore, David. *Mindfulness in the Marketplace*. Berkeley: Parallax, 2005.

Goethe, Ann. *Midnight Lemonade*. New York: Delacorte, 1994.

Green, Adam and Eleonore Stump. *Hidden Divinity and Religious Belief*. Cambridge: Cambridge University Press, 2016.

Hall, Donald. "My Son My Executioner." Poeticus. https://www.poeticous.com/donald-hall/my-son-my-executioner.

Hayden, Robert. "Those Winter Sundays." Poetry Foundation. https://www.poetryfoundation.org/poems/46461/those-winter-sundays.

Hillman, James. *The Essential James Hillman*. Abingdon-on-Thames: Routledge, 1990.

Jensen, Robert. *The End of Patriarchy*. Melbourne: Spinifex, 2017.

Kazanzakis, Nikos. *The Last Temptation of Christ*. Translated by Peter A. Bien. New York: Simon and Schuster, 1960.

King, Martin Luther, Jr. *Strength to Love*. Boston: Beacon Hill, 1963.

Lao Tzu. "Violence Always Rebounds Upon Oneself." *Content Catnip*, July 11, 2020. https://contentcatnip.com/2020/07/11/lao-tzu-violence-always-rebounds-upon-oneself/.

Levi, Primo. *Survival in Auschwitz*. New York: Simon & Schuster, 1966.

Love, Jan. "Practicing Consensus at the Table: Doing Democracy Differently." *Conflict and Communion*. Discipleship Resources, May 2006.

Luther, Martin. *The Letters of Martin Luther*. Classic Reprint, 1908.

Marcel, Gabriel. *Creative Fidelity*. Chestnut Ridge, NY: Crossroad, 1982.

Marlowe, Christopher. *The Tragedy of Doctor Faustus*. Cambridge, MA: Harvard Classics, 1909.

May, Gerald. *The Dark Night of the Soul*. New York: HarperCollins, 2004.

Merton, Thomas. *Thoughts in Solitude*. New York: Macmillan, 1956.

Milton, John. *Paradise Lost*. Poetry Foundation. https://www.poetryfoundation.org/poems/45718/paradise-lost-book-1-1674-version.

Muhaiyaddeen, Bawa. "Jihad: The Holy War Within." Bawa Muhainadden Fellowship. July 20, 2015. https://www.bmf.org/translations/jihad-the-holy-war-within/.

O'Connor, Flannery. *Letters of Flannery O'Connor*, ed. Sally Fitzgerald. New York: Vintage Books, 1979.

Palmer, Parker. *The Courage to Teach*. Hoboken: John Wiley and Sons, 1998.

Pascal, Blaise. *Internet Encyclopedia of Philosophy*. https://iep.utm.edu/.

Percy, Walker. *The Message in the Bottle*. New York: Farrar, Straus, and Giroux, 1975.

———. "Questions They Never Asked Me." *Humanities* 10, no. 3 (1989): 9–12.

———. *The Second Coming*. New York: Macmillan, 1980.

Peterson, Eugene. *Run with the Horses*. Downers Grove, IL: InterVarsity, 2019. https://www.goodreads.com.

Powell, Clark. "James Dickey (1923-1997) A Memory." *The Harbinger*, October 7, 1997. http://www.theharbinger.org/xvi/971007/clark.html.

"Prayer for Priests." https://www.catholic.org/prayers/prayer.php?p=1432.

Bibliography

Rabelais, Francois. *The Third Book of the Heroic Deeds and Sayings of the Good Pantagruel*. Encyclopedia.com. 2019. http://encyclopedia.com.

Redmoon, Ambrose. "No Peaceful Warriors." *Gnosis* (1991): 40–45.

Reed, Ishmael. *Writin' Is Fightin'*. Boston: Addison-Wesley, 1988.

Ribner, Irving and George Kittredge, eds. *The Complete Works of Shakespeare*. Hoboken: John Wiley and Sons, 1971.

Rohr, Richard. "Creation and Incarnation." *Global Catholic Climate Movement*, February 23, 2019. https://catholicclimatemovement.global/fr-richard-rohr-on-creation-and-incarnation/.

Sennett, Richard. "Cooperation." http://socialscience.com.

Shakya, Ming Zhen. "Zen and Money." Zen Buddhist Order of Hsu Yun. https://zbohy.zatma.org/Dharma/zbohy/Literature/essays/mzs/zen_and_money.html.

Spears, Ross, director. *To Render a Life*. Riverdale, MD: Agee Films, 1992. DVD.

Tennyson, Alfred Lord. "Ulysses." Poetry Foundation. https://www.poetryfoundation.org/poems/45392/ulysses.

Thoreau, Henry. *Walden*. Boston: Tickner and Fields, 1854.

Twain, Mark. *Letters from the Earth*. New York: Harper and Row, 1909.

"Who Will Buy a Poem?". Unknown. Ireland.

Williams, William Carlos. "The Widow's Lament in Springtime." Poetry Foundation. January 1922. https://www.poetryfoundation.org/poetrymagazine/browse?contentId=15468.

Woodman, Marion. "An Interview with Marion Woodman." *Parabola* (Summer 1987).

Wordsworth, William. "My Heart Leaps Up." https://poets.org/poem/my-heart-leaps.

Wyatt-Brown, Bertram. *The House of Percy*. New York: Oxford University Press, 1994.

Yeats, W. B. "Sailing to Byzantium." Poetry Foundation. https://www.poetryfoundation.org/poems/43291/sailing-to-byzantium.

———. "The Second Coming." Poetry Foundation. 1989. https://www.poetryfoundation.org/poems/43290/the-second-coming.

Zweig, Connie. "Becoming." *The Awakened Warrior*. New York: Putnam, 1994.

www.ingramcontent.com/pod-product-compliance
Lightning Source LLC
Chambersburg PA
CBHW050342230426
43663CB00010B/1956